WITHDRAWN AND OFFERED FOR SALE

© Haynes Publishing 2018
Published October 2018

A CIP Catalogue record for this book
is available from the British Library.

ISBN: 978 1 78521 567 4 (print)
       978 1 78521 609 1 (eBook)

Library of Congress control no. 2018950621

Published by Haynes Publishing,
Sparkford, Yeovil, Somerset BA22 7JJ
Tel: 01963 440635
Int. tel: +44 1963 440635
Website: www.haynes.com

Printed in Malaysia.

Bluffer's Guide®, Bluffer's® and Bluff Your Way®
are registered trademarks.

Series Editor: David Allsop.
Front cover illustration by Alan Capel.

CONTENTS

𝕭

'You have to be smart enough to understand the game, and dumb enough to think it's important.'

US Senator Eugene McCarthy

EARLY DOORS

Never before has the ability to bluff your way in football been as vital as it is now. From boardroom to building site, from wine bar to pub, every other conversation seems to be about the game. The smartest dinner parties, which once echoed with talk of Plato and the Old Vic, now concern themselves with Messi and Old Trafford. In short, if you cannot talk about football, you cannot take part in modern life.*

If you know that the expression 'early doors' derives from the world of theatre (as in a matinée performance), then you understand more than most footballers and football fans. But you must also realise that it is much better known as a football-related term for the beginning of a game, or indeed any undertaking, as in: 'We've got to make sure that we get stuck in early doors.'

So not only must you never be 'late doors', you must be properly prepared as you step through them. If you attempt to improvise in the jungle of trivia, invective and emotion that characterises modern football, you will soon be caught out. For proof of just how easily this can happen, you need look no further than the political world. Former prime minister Tony Blair, for example, was asked in a BBC radio interview about his 'lifelong' support of Newcastle United. A local newspaper went on to misreport the interview, claiming that Blair said he had fond teenage memories of watching legendary player Jackie Milburn, who had actually retired when Blair was four. The myth surrounding this 'claim', however, will take much longer to retire – if it ever does. Football fans can detect the whiff of phoniness from a great distance, and if there's one thing they all agree on, it's to hold in contempt anyone who claims to be a fervent supporter of a particular club when they're demonstrably not. Another prime minister, David Cameron, discovered this in 2015 when after years of claiming to be an Aston Villa fan he urged people to support West Ham. He described the incident as a 'brain fade', though many of those mocking him on social media pointed out that his confusion probably arose because the two teams wear the same colours (claret and blue).

Another case in point is Salman Rushdie who once wrote a magazine article professing his long-held love for Tottenham Hotspur in which he praised their legendary Scottish manager Bill Nicholson. Nicholson was in fact English.

So, as a bluffer you would be advised to follow the instructions given out by thousands of football managers through the years:

work hard in training;

keep your eye on the ball; and

don't do anything stupid.

In particular, you should remember the words of another politician, US Senator Eugene McCarthy, who compared his job to being involved in football (albeit the American version): 'You have to be smart enough to understand the game, and dumb enough to think it's important.' Admitting to a lack of understanding about the world's most popular spectator sport is the cultural equivalent to having a bad case of leprosy (in its advanced, pustulent phase).

This book sets out to guide you through the main danger zones encountered in football discussions, and to equip you with a vocabulary and an evasive technique that will minimise the risk of being rumbled as a bluffer. It will lend you a few easy-to-learn hints and methods that will allow you to be accepted as a football aficionado of rare ability and experience. But it will do more. It will give you the tools to impress legions of marvelling listeners with your knowledge and insight about 'the beautiful game' – without anyone discovering that before reading it you didn't know the difference between a 'hairdryer' and 'handbags at dawn'.

* Gender matters: It should be made clear that wherever in this book the impression is given that all football fans, players and officials are male, it is for reasons of grammatical convenience. It is not intended to suggest that men are more likely than women to have a keener grasp of the game. And if you should fall into that trap just remind yourself of the fate of 'expert' Sky football presenters Richard Keys and Andy Gray who were required to step down after a notorious sexism row when they questioned the job suitability of female Premier League assistant referee Sian Massey (who clearly knows more about the offside rule than most men).

The jewel in any bluffer's crown is the ability to explain the offside rule.

RULES OF ENGAGEMENT

The first recorded mention of football was over 2,000 years ago in China. The Yellow Emperor is said to have developed his soldiers' leg muscles by making them play with a stone football. References to heading the ball are notable by their absence.

It has been said that sport is a continuation of war by other means. For much of its history, football has tended to forget about the 'by other means' bit. Games in the British Isles were for centuries little more than an excuse for mass fights, with hundreds of players on each side. The residents of Chester are said to have celebrated victory over the marauding Danes by playing football with the head of a defeated opponent. This attitude to the sport continues to this day among the supporters of Millwall Football Club.

The rules of football were first formalised at Cambridge University in 1846, when Messrs H. de Winton and J.C. Thring met to decide a unified code for the game. Their deliberations took just under eight hours, thereby establishing the tradition that football should always be talked about for far longer than it takes to actually play the game. This tradition lives on with Sky TV's post-match analyses.

The first meeting of the Football Association (FA) was on 26 October 1863 at the Freemasons' Tavern in London's Covent Garden, near the headquarters of the Freemasons. The bluffer might admit to holding a suitably jaundiced view of the FA, pointing out the irony of its early connection to an organisation famed for its secretive practices and refusal to explain itself to the outside world.

The world game is now governed by FIFA, the International Federation of Association Football. The fact that these initials are in the wrong order tells you everything you need to know about this organisation. (Admittedly the French name is actually Fédération Internationale de Football Association, but why spoil a good story?) Never overburdened by headlines claiming that their procedures are completely above board and utterly legitimate, FIFA's biggest brush with scandal came during the bidding process for the 2022 World Cup. Having weighed up the respective bids of the various countries competing to host the tournament, Sepp Blatter (the body's then president) announced that he and his cronies – sorry, well-respected fellow bureaucrats – had decided on Qatar. The fact that this former British protectorate sounds like a medical complaint is the least of its worries when it comes to being taken seriously as a home for football's biggest showpiece. There are issues concerning the country's policies on human rights, freedom of the press and – most crucially – the availability of alcohol. But the main practical problem is that in June and July (when the World Cup is always held) Qatar is so hot that players and fans could suffer serious dehydration (especially if the English supporters are deprived of their prescribed ingestion of generous quantities of lager). One suggestion was that leagues around the world could take a mid-season break to allow the World Cup to run during the winter. You can imagine how well those leagues responded to that. Your line on this is that the World Cup should be awarded to countries that have a tried-and-trusted record of hosting it, and are conspicuously good at hosting big sporting events such as the Olympics; to pick one utterly at random… oh, let's take for example…England. In the months of June and July, countries like Qatar might, meanwhile, be better left to host the world 'Frying an Egg on the Bonnet of a Car' championship.

KICKING THE BLADDER

Those who wish to deride football always refer to it as 22 grown men kicking an inflated pig's bladder around a field. The bluffer, on the other hand, knows that the very essence of football is that it is 22 grown men kicking an inflated pig's bladder around a field. If they happen to be 'professional' footballers, they will probably be paid vast amounts of money for kicking a bladder around. This deeply irks most non-professional footballers and football fans. But they learn to live with it, as they also learn to live with the knowledge that the conjunction of the words 'professional' and 'footballer' is essentially an oxymoron.

Very little needs to be known about the rules. Whichever set of 11 men kicks the bladder between the posts at the other end of the field the most often, most often wins. The game really is that simple. Why else do you think Paul Gascoigne was so good at it?

The only rules of football with which it is necessary to be familiar are those that govern how long the pig's bladder should be kicked around the field, and what happens when it stops being kicked around the field.

STOPPAGES IN PLAY

The throw-in
This occurs when the ball runs over one of the long sides of the pitch (the 'touchline'). The last team to touch the ball concede to their opponents the right to throw it back on. One of the opposing players picks up the ball then surreptitiously edges further and further along the line in an attempt to gain territorial advantage until the referee loses patience and orders him to take the throw-in from where the ball actually crossed the line.

The goal kick
This occurs when the ball runs over one of the short sides of the pitch, where the goals are situated (the 'goal line'). If the last team to touch the ball was the team

attacking the goal at that end, they concede to their opponents the right to kick the ball back up the other end. This task is normally undertaken by the goalkeeper. You will know that your keeper is having a particularly bad game when he can't even get the ball to reach the halfway line before it rolls slowly off the pitch, thereby giving your opponents a throw-in.

The corner

This occurs when the last team to touch the ball before it crossed the goal line is the team defending the goal at that end. They then concede to their opponents the right to kick the ball back on from the corner of the pitch. Two things always happen at a corner. Firstly, the player taking it kicks the ball in the general direction of the goal, so that his teammates can try to score. And, secondly, the opposition fans clustered behind him make intimidating remarks about his haircut/recent drink-driving conviction/wife's sexual proclivities.

The free kick

This occurs when a player commits a 'foul' (*see* below). There are two types: the 'direct' free kick, when a goal can be scored directly from the kick, and the 'indirect' free kick when it must be touched by a second member of the same team before a goal can be scored. The type of free kick awarded depends on the gravity of offence committed, but in both cases the fouled-against team is allowed to kick the ball from the point at which the foul took place, and all members of the team whose player committed the foul must retreat at least 10 yards.

That is 10 football yards, a distance which used to be roughly equivalent to eight and a half normal yards. Players, especially when the free kick was near their own goal, wanted to be as close to the ball as possible to prevent it going into that goal. So as soon as the referee had awarded a free kick, he paced out 10 yards in the direction of the goal, and waited for the wall of opposing players to edge back towards him. This process occured at the rate of one inch per 15 seconds until the nearest player was in touching distance of him, at which point he could let the free kick be taken without losing too much face. Eventually tiring of this charade, the game's authorities introduced vanishing foam. This is contained in a can, and sprayed by the referee on to the pitch. He puts a small dot at the point where the free kick has been awarded, then paces 10 yards towards the goal and sprays a line. The opposition wall has to remain behind this line. The foam disappears after about 60 seconds, so ensuring the game isn't marred by dots, lines and doodles all over the pitch. An early version of the foam was proposed by England legend Bobby Charlton in the 1980s, but the authorities did nothing about it. Probably because they thought Charlton was banging on about the hairspray with which he fixed his Trump-like legendary comb-over in place.

A player may voluntarily waive the 10-yard rule himself if he thinks that by taking the free kick quickly he can catch the opposition unawares. More often than not, though, such attempts are likely to catch his own side unawares as well, resulting in an argument as to whose fault it was that the free kick was wasted, during which the opposition go up the other end and score.

If a foul has been committed, the referee might sometimes 'play the advantage'. This happens when he decides that the team whose player was fouled has more to gain by carrying on with the game than by stopping to take a free kick. In such circumstances, the team sometimes go on to score a goal, in which case the referee is praised for his common sense and foresight. But usually they don't, and the referee is berated for not giving them the free kick in the first place.

THE SET PIECE

Set pieces are pre-prepared routines that sides employ when awarded a free kick. They will have been practised on the training ground to the point where every single player knows his role by heart. They will then be re-enacted in the match and, inevitably, will bear absolutely no relation to the carefully rehearsed routine in training. Players and fans alike will watch in open-mouthed amazement as the ball passes harmlessly over everyone's head and bounces off the electronic scoreboard.

Similar advance planning goes into corners. Teams will rehearse a number of options, for which coded signals can then be given to his teammates by the player taking the corner. For instance:

- Raising his right hand before he takes it might mean: 'I'm going to kick this straight out of play before it even reaches the near goalpost, thereby wasting the corner and making you deeply disappointed.'

- Raising his left hand might mean: 'I'm going to kick this straight to their goalkeeper, who'll then be able to boot it right up the field for a goal while you lot are still shouting at me for squandering our chance.'

Solo set pieces are also used. These usually involve 'curl' (or what used to be known as a 'banana' or 'screw shot') and involve bending or swerving the ball around the opposition players giving the goalkeeper little chance of saving it. Well, that's the idea anyway. The effect is achieved by imparting spin on the ball as you kick it. Ex-Arsenal player Thierry Henry was an acknowledged master of this extremely difficult skill, as was the Brazilian Roberto Carlos, whose curled free kick against France in 1997 amazed everyone watching the match. It also led to a surge in business for glaziers, as schoolboys all over the world attempted to recreate the free kick in their back gardens.

THE PENALTY

Around each goal is marked a 'penalty area' (also known as 'the box'). If a player commits a foul inside his own area, he concedes a penalty kick to the opposition.

After the referee has rid himself of the fouling player (and all his teammates protesting about the decision – which normally takes about 20 minutes), he places the ball on the penalty spot, which is directly in front of the goal, 12 yards out. Any member of the team awarded the penalty may then step forward to take it. He and the goalkeeper attempting to save the penalty are the only two players allowed inside the box until the ball has been struck.

What commentators seldom refer to is the penalty-taker's marathon *Call of Duty* video game session which only ended at six o'clock that morning.

The goal is 24 feet across and 8 feet high. Until the penalty-taker has kicked the ball, the goalkeeper is not allowed to advance off his line. In such circumstances, you would think it impossible to miss a penalty. But somehow professional footballers, whose very existence depends on their supposed ability to kick a ball, when faced with the task of aiming a ball at 192 square feet of space protected by only one man blocking approximately 12 square feet of space, manage week in, week out either to have the kick saved or to miss the target completely.

Commentators normally excuse players missing penalties with reference to the pressure, the sheer weight of expectation placed on them by their teammates and supporters, the exposure of human frailty inevitable when two combatants glow incandescent in the crucible of sporting drama. What commentators seldom refer to is the penalty-taker's marathon *Call of Duty* video game session which only ended at six o'clock that morning.

FOULS

Fouls fall into two main categories:

1. Fouls against a member of the opposition

This normally boils down to playing your opponent instead of the ball. You might think this equates to tripping him up. But you'd be wrong. Footballers, despite their intellectual inadequacies in other areas of life, are surprisingly cunning when it comes to fouling an opponent. They can disguise their foul as:

- **a mistimed tackle** ('I'm terribly sorry, was my foot a fraction of a second late there, causing it to connect not with the ball but with your shinbone?');

- **an attempt to stay on their feet** ('Oh I say, what a shame that in stretching out my arm to maintain my balance I inadvertently placed my elbow at high speed into your eye socket'); or

- **a keen interest in fashion** ('On the contrary, the reason I was holding on to the back of your shirt was not to prevent you reaching the ball and scoring a goal, but to see if the shirt really is as silky-smooth as it looks').

2. Fouls against a specific law of the game

The most common such foul is 'offside'. This is the cause of so much confusion that it merits its own section (*see* page 21). Other fouls of this type include:

- **Handball** The key here is intent. If a player (other than a goalkeeper inside his own penalty area) deliberately controls the ball with his hand, it is deemed a foul. If the referee judges the contact accidental, no foul is awarded. But you need not concern yourself with such distinctions. If the player involved is on your team, it is not a foul. If he is on the opposition team, it is, and you should join in with your fellow supporters' ritualistic cry of '–'andball!', followed by a stream of profanities directed at the referee if he declines to award a free kick (*see* 'Diego Maradona', page 78).

- **The back pass** This was a law introduced in 1992 to counter the problem of teams protecting their lead at the end of a game by continually passing the ball back to their goalkeeper. It is now illegal for a goalkeeper to pick up the ball if it has been kicked (as opposed to headed or chested) to him by one of his teammates. As well as making for more exciting, attacking football, this rule change has given goalkeepers – paranoid souls at the best of times – yet another reason for moaning that no one likes them and that the whole game is stacked against them.

- **The six-second rule** Another rule change from the 1990s, to 'speed up the game', states that the goalkeeper must not hold on to the ball for longer than six seconds after receiving it. (Previously he could hold on to it for longer, but was not allowed to take more than four steps while doing so.)

As a result, goalkeepers had to develop the ability to drop the ball and control it with their feet. This necessitated a level of footballing skill and fitness that many of them did not previously possess.

BOOKINGS

The referee and/or his two linesmen (*see* pages 103–4) occasionally manage to spot fouls when they occur. If the offence is a particularly bad one, in addition to awarding a free kick, the referee may caution the offending player by showing him a yellow card. (This is also known as 'booking' him, because the referee notes the caution in his book.) A second yellow card in one match results in a red card, and the player involved is sent off. He must then leave the field of play, angrily kicking several water bottles along the touchline as he does so. This is a sign to his team's supporters that he disagrees emphatically with the referee's decision.

For particularly violent tackles, or if a player raises his arm to hit an opponent, the referee may send a player off without showing him the first yellow card. A notoriously unforgiving midfielder called Vinnie Jones received this sanction so often that towards the end of his career they usually started running his bath just after the match started. (*See* 'Early bath' in 'Glossary'). Another 'competitive' player of this type was the absurdly coiffured Leicester City, Derby County, Birmingham City and Blackburn Rovers midfielder Robbie Savage. As if his surname wasn't clue enough, he also took part in the TV show *Strictly Come Dancing,* providing yet another opportunity to call him a talentless 'hoofer'.

However, if you want factual back-up for your nomination of the most violent player in Premier League history, choose Lee Bowyer (pronounced 'bo–ya', though it should perhaps have been 'chop-ya-in-half'), whose clubs included Leeds United, Newcastle United and West Ham United. (United is what most fans were in seeing him as a somewhat over-competitive, unguided missile.) Several years after his retirement he is still near the top of the table of most yellow cards received in the Premier League. The figure is either 99 or 100, depending on whether you count the two yellows that lead to a red as separate cards. Some statisticians don't, you see. Throw that into the conversation: it's precisely the sort of arcane statistical debate that has most football fans wetting themselves in excitement.

THE OFFSIDE RULE

The jewel in any bluffer's crown is the ability to explain the offside rule. It is famous for being very simple to understand (unless you are a Premier League linesman) but very hard to describe.

Never ever attempt to explain the offside rule at a dinner party using wine glasses and salt cellars to represent players. Others before you have tried and ruined not just their evenings but their marriages in the process. These attempts normally start with someone setting up one side of a place mat to symbolise the goal line. They end, several hours later, with at least one member of the party in the bathroom crying and everyone else standing around the table screaming things like, 'No, the pepper pot is the defender, you moron!'

The real trick to explaining the offside rule is first to explain why it was introduced. It was to counter the problem of 'goalhanging', where one attacker simply stands on the opposition's goal line, waiting for the ball to be knocked forward to him, which allows him to score the simplest and least challenging of goals. (At this point you can, with a knowing smile, add the phrase 'no names, Gary Lineker'.)

Once this fact has been grasped, everything else falls into place. At the moment the ball is played forward to an attacker, he must have at least two opposition players (normally the goalkeeper and a defender) between himself and the goal line. Otherwise he is deemed to be offside, and a free kick is granted to the opposition.

Teams playing a defensive style of football can take advantage of this rule to 'spring the offside trap'. This is when the entire defence moves forward at the very last moment, thereby stranding the attacker with only the goalkeeper ahead of him. All the defenders then raise their right arms to appeal to the linesman. The Arsenal team of the 1980s became so adept at this tactic that their back four usually looked like the front row of a Nuremberg rally.

In recent years the rule has been altered subtly to allow someone to be in an offside position as long as he isn't 'actively involved in play'. This broadly means either that he's not trying to score, or is not distracting the attention of a defender who would otherwise be dealing with the attacker who really is trying to score. In practice, the whole question is clouded in uncertainty and obfuscation (a word little used by professional footballers). If required to deliver a verdict on whether a player was 'actively involved in play', raise a cynical eyebrow and venture: 'As much as he ever is.' This can be the bluffer's refinement of a comment by the legendary Nottingham Forest manager Brian Clough: 'If a player isn't interfering with play then he shouldn't be on the pitch.'

LENGTH OF A MATCH

A football match consists of two 45-minute halves. In addition, 'stoppage time' (aka 'added' time, usually measured quite unscientifically between one and four minutes) is added on at the end of each half in a vague attempt to make up for the time that has been wasted during play. The long-serving Manchester United manager Sir Alex Ferguson became famous for checking officials' assessment of this time, to the point where he was rumoured to be sponsored by Accurist. Intriguingly, keen observers noticed a pattern in his insistence that there was always too much time added when his team was winning, and too little when it was losing. This curious phenomenon became known as 'Fergie Time'.

An experiment was once undertaken at a football match to discover just how much time had been frittered away. It was found that the ball had been in play for 43 of the 90 minutes. How those conducting the experiment had managed to pick a match with quite so much genuine action in it remains a mystery, but the discrepancy is easy to explain. Whichever side was in the lead at any given point would have minimised the time remaining for their opponents to equalise by:

- rolling around on the grass pretending to be injured, a tactic perfected by Luis Suarez of Barcelona at the time of writing, Neymar currently of Paris Saint-Germain, Cristiano Ronaldo currently of Juventus, and just about any other striker you can think of including the daddy-of-them-all, Jürgen Klinsmann;

- letting the ball remain stationary on the ground after it has gone out of play before finally taking the goalkick, throw-in, etc.; and

- substituting players, who saunter slowly off the pitch so their replacements have to wait to come on.

Their opponents would have complained vigorously to the referee about time-wasting until they themselves took the lead, after which they would have indulged in exactly the same practices.

If, in a knock-out cup competition, the scores are level at the end of 90 minutes and the match has to be decided there and then (in other words, if a replay is not an option), there are two possibilities available:

1. Extra time

This is a further period of play, comprising two halves of 15 minutes each. Towards the end of the second half of extra time, the players will have been running around for nearly two hours. As a result their legs will be like jelly, and their brains like blancmange (no change there, then). This is when you will witness some of the most entertainingly incompetent football imaginable.

2. Penalty shoot-out

This will take place if neither team has won at the end of extra time. Each side takes five penalty kicks, after which, if no kicks have been missed and the match has still not been decided, the penalties continue until one side scores and the other misses. You will easily recognise a fan who has recently attended a match decided by a penalty shoot-out: he will have no fingernails. Unless he's English, that is. They don't bother with the nail-biting because they know their team is usually going to lose. This isn't just the innate pessimism associated with the country's national character. It's based on hard evidence: England have lost all but two of the international penalty shoot-outs in which they've been involved. The exceptions were at the 1996 European Championship, when they managed to scrape past Spain, and then in the 2018 World Cup when they managed to scrape past Colombia. Apart from that they have lost in World Cups to Germany (1990), Argentina (1998) and Portugal (2006), and in European Championships to Germany (1996), Portugal (2004) and Italy (2012). (For more details on some of these shoot-outs *see* 'Total Football', though if you're English it's probably not a good idea.) Such is the pattern that whenever fans mention the famous football game that took place between English and German soldiers in 'No Man's Land' during the 1914 Christmas Day truce in the First World War, someone inevitably suggests that the Germans must have won on penalties. In fact, the game was just an informal kickabout, with no result as such. As ever, though, we recommend not letting the facts get in the way of a good story.

BLUFFER'S TIP *Casually throw in the fact that* 12 Yard, *the TV production company behind the BBC quiz show* Eggheads, *is so called because the programme's final 'winner takes all' section equates to a penalty shoot-out, the penalty spot being 12 yards out from goal. You'll make yourself look a cultural giant – for many football fans,* Eggheads *is virtually Chekhov.*

VAR

Forget everything you formerly knew and loved about contentious refereeing decisions. Now there is even more potential for controversy and accusations of incompetence. The video assistant referee (VAR) system, pronounced "Vee-Ay-Ar" (and nothing else) is a means of reviewing the head referee's decisions (or absence of them) during the match and now appears to be firmly entrenched in the laws of the game. After trials in a number of competitions around the world, it made its full debut at the 2018 World Cup. According to FIFA, 99.3 per cent of "match-changing" decisions were called correctly after review. Clearly, the hotly disputed 'handball' apparently committed by Croatia in the final against France was one that slipped through the net. *Plus ça change* as the new world champions might say.

On the other hand earlier in the same competition two goals were correctly given after being initially ruled offside, including one by South Korea that helped to eliminate world champions Germany. So what's not to like?

TAKING A POSITION

The easiest place to watch or play a game of football is your local park on a Sunday morning. However, advice to those thinking of playing park football is simple: don't. This is not because the other players will be better than you. It is precisely because they won't. Where skill is absent, violence finds a home.

It should be noted, though, that watching park football appeals to the romantic in every football fan. Standards are much more relaxed than in the professional game, so participants wear whatever kit they want to. As a result, you will frequently witness bizarre events like a Crewe Alexandra striker scoring against a Barcelona goalkeeper. These sights help to keep alive the fan's dream that every underdog will have its day.

If you insist on playing the game yourself, we strongly advise that you eschew park football and stick to more solitary displays of footballing skill, in particular 'keepie-uppie'. This is where you bounce the ball off your feet, knees, head, shoulders and (if you're really clever) off the chest and the back of the neck (not at the same time, obviously), so preventing it from hitting the ground. But be warned: it is deceptively difficult. Professional footballers, as they warm up before a match, give the impression that keepie-uppie is easy. Try it yourself and you will realise why they are professional footballers. (The question does arise as to why English players can perform incredible keepie-uppie during the warm-up, then fail to hit an open goal from three yards during the match itself.) Never try keepie-uppie near a window.

There is film footage of the great Argentinian footballer Diego Maradona playing keepie-uppie with a golf ball (when he wasn't quite as rotund as he is today). Do not watch this clip if you have recently been practising your technique. You will, as hundreds have before you, weep bitter tears of frustration.

A footballer's high physical intelligence comes at a price: it tends to intrude into the pathways used for verbal skills.

Happily, you need never apologise for your poor footballing skills. Instead, refer to your relatively low PIQ (Physical Intelligence Quotient). Scientists now suggest that agility of the kind displayed by professional footballers is due to their brains being wired in such a way as to maximise the coordination of intention, muscle, motor and perception skills. However, this high physical intelligence comes at a price: it tends to intrude into the pathways used for verbal skills. So while they are adept at stringing lots of passes together (unless they're from the British Isles), you prefer being able to string sentences together.

POSITIONS

Goalkeeper
This is the player who stands between the goalposts, attempting to stop the opposition from scoring. Often referred to as the 'goalie' or the 'keeper', he differs from outfield players in two respects. He is:

- the only player allowed to handle the ball (as long as he is inside his own penalty area); and

- normally the only player near enough to the crowd behind the goal to be pelted with small household objects.

Two principal characteristics are needed to be a successful goalie. You must be tall (so that your outstretched hand can reach the ball) and clinically insane (so that your concentration on putting outstretched hand to ball isn't disturbed by opposition players' knees rearranging your facial features). The Coventry City goalkeeper Steve Ogrizovic reportedly had his nose broken no fewer than 12 times during his career. Fortunately his looks to begin with were such that this did not greatly matter.

The most famous case of goalkeeper bravery came during the 1956 FA Cup Final, in which Manchester City's Bert Trautmann played the last quarter of an hour with a broken neck. (Get bonus bluffing points for knowing the name of the Birmingham City player whose knee did the damage: Peter Murphy, known – with typical footballing ingenuity – as 'Spud' Murphy.) Although Trautmann was in great pain (he had to play on because this was the era before substitutions were allowed), it didn't become clear for a couple of days that his neck was actually broken. Nonetheless, his discomfort was clear even as he collected his winner's medal from Prince Philip, who expressed noticeable sympathy. Trautmann was in fact a former German prisoner of war, and a recipient of the Iron Cross for his bravery as a Luftwaffe paratrooper on the Eastern Front. Declining repatriation to Germany at the end of the war, he worked as a farmhand in Lancashire before joining St Helen's Town and then Manchester City as goalkeeper. Stoically withstanding initial protests from fans, he eventually became the most popular German in Britain (and has arguably never been eclipsed), and in 2004 he was awarded an honorary OBE. It's an odd thing about football; despite being full of overpaid preening prima donnas guilty of the most inexcusable gamesmanship, it can still remind you that it once valued things like valour and nobility.

A useful piece of information for the bluffer to slip into conversation is that both Pope John Paul II and opera tenor Luciano Pavarotti were quite handy goalkeepers in their younger days. One of them had to move around considerably more than the other to stop the ball getting past him. In fact, there are quite a few celebrity keepers you can throw into the mix. Spanish crooner Julio Iglesias stood 'between the sticks' (as the position is sometimes called by fans). Arthur Conan Doyle played under the pseudonym 'A.C. Smith'. The philosopher Albert Camus played in his native Algeria, saying: 'All that I know most surely about morality and obligations, I owe to football.' Vladimir Nabokov kept goal during his time at Cambridge University, while Che Guevara also reputedly occupied the position as a university medical student. (Those who would have dearly loved to see him playing on the left wing were denied by the charismatic revolutionary's health – he chose to play in goal because of his asthma.)

Those who have kept goal professionally before going on to find fame in other fields include self-professed 'Son of the Godhead', conspiracy theorist and former co-presenter of *Grandstand* David Icke (Coventry City youth team, then Hereford United), and Gordon Ramsay (Glasgow Rangers) – although this is disputed by the club, which says he might have briefly been a triallist (but don't bank on it).

Centre backs

Also known as centre halves, these are the two players who stand immediately in front of the goalkeeper, in the centre of defence. In long-standing pairings, centre backs can develop an almost telepathic ability to operate as a unit. The taller one jumps up to head the ball, while the shorter one stands on the toes of the opposition player to prevent him doing likewise.

Centre backs often make good team captains – the former Chelsea and England player John Terry, for example. (Any problems he had with hanging on to the England captaincy were due to off-the-field 'incidents'.) This is partly because their position on the pitch is a good one from which to command players, and partly because they are usually physically imposing and often psychopathic. These latter qualities also help explain why they never get shouted at by teammates when they make mistakes.

Full backs
These are the two defenders who operate outside the centre backs. They are also referred to as 'left back' and 'right back'. Their tactics for countering the opposition usually fall into one of two categories. There is the 'No One Ever Scored from Row Z' approach, where the ball is kicked into the crowd at the earliest opportunity. And there is the 'Player or Ball' approach, which dictates that full backs are happy for an opposition player to go past them, or for the ball to go past them – but never both at the same time.

Wing backs
An alternative defensive arrangement is to have three centre backs and two defenders outside them who are referred to as 'wing backs'. Their role is twofold. They push forward and attack down the wings (the edges

of the pitch), and are the players whom the rest of the team blame when the opposition get past them and cross the ball in for a goal.

Midfielders

These are the four or five players operating between the defenders and the attackers. They assist both in equal measure in that they give the defence someone to criticise for never running back to help them, and the attackers someone to blame for never getting the ball forward so that they can score.

In addition, midfielders tend to be the players nearest to the referee, which means they have a crucial intimidatory role to perform should the ref be thinking of sending anyone off.

BLUFFER'S TIP *Refer to a particularly energetic midfielder as a 'box to box' player – they are constantly switching from defensive play in their own penalty area to attacking play in the opposition's.*

Centre forwards

These are the players who hang around in the opposition penalty area ensuring that their hair remains neat enough for tomorrow's promotional photo shoot. Occasionally, and if they happen to be in the right place, they might deign to knock the ball into the goal, as long as doing so doesn't get mud over the sponsor's name on their boot. They are also, to a man, proficient divers (*see* 'Glossary', page 120). Especially if someone hits them with a feather.

OTHER FORMS OF THE GAME

To enjoy the excitement of playing the game competitively without risking life and limb, many football fans used to opt for the tabletop game Subbuteo. This was also used by real-life managers to illustrate tactical theories to their players. Obviously, wooden figures with limited movement and zero intelligence have their limitations in this regard – but the footballers do their best to understand.

These days younger fans – and indeed many of the older ones – prefer their football simulations on screen. The 'FIFA' series of video games, updated every year and available for consoles such as the PlayStation and Xbox, are played for hours on end by supporters around the world. Not just supporters, either – many professional footballers are fans of the game too. Lionel Messi – widely agreed to be the best player in the world – has been reported as spending up to three hours a day playing video games. Which is ironic, as the long-serving Arsenal manager Arsène Wenger said Messi's on-field prowess was so great he was 'like a PlayStation player'.

If you want to be a manager rather than a player, the 'fantasy football league' schemes operated by many newspapers and websites provide the ideal opportunity. These allow you to construct an imaginary team from real professional players whose performances on the field then earn your 'side' points. This exactly replicates the experience of being a football manager – apart, that is, from:

- the constant calls in the press for your resignation;

- the need to conduct your team talks in seven different languages so your foreign stars can understand you; and

- the frustration of dealing with a chairman who wants to spend all his money on the stadium's new hotel and leisure complex instead of giving it to you to buy more players.

The oldest way for football fans to indulge their passion for the game is entering the 'spot-the-ball' competition in local newspapers. (Hint: This gives them the chance to place the ball exactly where they want it to be – something very few of the players can manage.)

Midfielders give the defence someone to criticise for never running back to help them, and the attackers someone to blame for never getting the ball forward so that they can score.

SILVERWARE

The trophies awarded in football competitions are nearly always known as 'silverware' when any British team is taking part. If you call them anything else you will reveal ignorance on a bluff-exposing scale. Footballers love using the term, and are prone to making profound observations such as: 'No matter how much silverware you win, it is never enough.' This is designed to give the impression that there's already a handsome collection of silverware in a bulging trophy cabinet.

The following are the principal competitions in which the most desirable silverware is keenly fought for:

DOMESTIC COMPETITIONS

The Premier League

This is the most important competition in English football. The top 20 teams in England and Wales play each other twice (home and away). You get three points for a win, one for a draw and none for losing. At the end of the season (which runs from August until May), the points from all 38 games are added together. The same few names always finish at the top. The only interest left in the Premier League is who will get relegated. Relegation is the terrible fate that awaits the bottom three sides. They must play their next season in the division below (the Football League Championship) which lies on the edge of the footballing map.

When early May comes around, those who normally struggle to check that their change is right at the supermarket become experts at mental arithmetic.

If two sides have finished the season with the same number of points, the concept of goal difference is employed to decide who finishes above the other. The total number of goals conceded in all matches is subtracted from the total number of goals scored, and whichever team has the better goal difference is awarded the higher place. This means that, as the end of the season approaches, fans of teams threatened with relegation are usually seen engaging in complicated calculations of which results are necessary for their team to stay up (or 'avoid the drop' as it is often called): 'If we win each of our last three matches four-nil, and City draw one match and lose the other two three-nil, we can stay up. As long as Rovers don't win by any more than two on the last day of the season, unless United…'

So inspired do football supporters become by the game that when early May comes around, those who normally struggle to check that their change is right at the supermarket become experts at mental arithmetic.

One of the most thrilling finishes to a season in English football history came in the 2011–12 Premier League. Going into the final matches, fierce rivals Manchester United and Manchester City were level on points, City having a better goal difference. United won their match, meaning that as long as City did likewise both teams would get three points and City's goal difference would win them the title. But with time nearly up, City trailed their opponents (Queens Park Rangers) 2–1. Even though they scored in the second minute of added time, this still wasn't enough – they were only drawing, and they needed a win. The Manchester United players, whose match had finished, waited on the pitch for news…and were sick as parrots (*see* 'Glossary') when City managed to score a winning goal in the fourth minute of added time (the 'last kick of the game') so bagging themselves the title.

BLUFFER'S TIP *A useful fact to deploy when finishing places are being discussed is the question of what would happen if two teams (either those chasing the title or trying to avoid relegation) were to finish level on points, goal difference and goals scored. Most fans (even seasoned ones) assume that the teams' results in their two matches against each other would decide the issue. Not so: they would take part in a play-off* *match. It's highly unlikely that this mathematical situation will ever occur, but that doesn't matter. By highlighting this little-known gem, you'll lead everyone to assume that you really do know your football.*

The Football League Championship

In 1992 the old First Division (then the game's top flight) renamed itself the Premier League and the Second Division renamed itself the First Division; then, at the start of the 2004/5 season, the First Division (formerly the Second Division) renamed itself the Football League Championship. Wake up at the back please.

Dropping down from the Premier League to the Championship means you lose millions in TV rights, and all your temperamental Brazilian signings decide they don't want to play in front of 5,000 people on a rainy Wednesday night in Norwich, so transfer to one of the teams who have been promoted from the Championship to take your place.

Below the Championship are the divisions known as League One and League Two. Until 2004 these were known as the Second and Third Divisions, which before 1992 were known as the Third and Fourth Divisions. It is rumoured that football is also played in these divisions, although evidence of this in the modern media is hard to find – and this is not just because the press cannot remember which division is which.

The FA Cup

This is not just the most famous knockout football competition in the world; it is also responsible for generating more clichés than the rest of sport put together. These include:

- 'The great leveller';
- 'The magic/romance of the Cup';
- 'Dreaming of the twin towers';
- 'David against Goliath'; and
- 'A giant-killing act they'll be talking about for years.'

You will gather from these phrases that the Football Association Challenge Cup is open to all clubs, from the smallest non-league band of accountants and mechanics to the most successful teams in the Premier League. The third round, played in January, is the first round in which the biggest clubs compete, and is often referred to as 'the most romantic day in football'. This statement loses some of its power, however, when you remember that the average footballer's idea of romance is taking a picture of himself naked and texting it to a prospective girlfriend.

For most of its history, the FA Cup Final has been played at Wembley (hence the now-demolished 'twin towers' of which so many dreams were made). The first final held there was the so-called 'White Horse' match of 1923, famous for an estimated crowd of 300,000 people spilling on to the pitch and having to be restrained by PC George Scorey on his horse Billy. Not many people know that when Billy died several years later the Metropolitan Police presented Scorey with one of the horse's hooves, polished and mounted. How extraordinarily touching.

The temporary removal (in 2001) of football's showpiece match from its traditional home was the cause of great consternation, not least because fans could no longer indulge in the chant first popularised by Tottenham Hotspur: 'Ossie's going to Wembley, his knees have gone all trembly' (a paean to their Argentinian midfield maestro Osvaldo Ardiles courtesy of 'rockney' combo Chas 'n' Dave). Now that the fixture is back in its spiritual home, all is well again. Even though the demands of Premier League and European Champions League matches now mean that some bigger clubs don't take the FA Cup as seriously as they once did, the final retains a number of time-honoured traditions, and it is advisable that you familiarise yourself with them:

- The match is always attended by a member of the Royal Family who has no interest in or knowledge of football and makes no attempt whatsoever to disguise that fact.*

- The match is always attended by a senior politician who has no interest in or knowledge of football and makes every attempt to disguise that fact. Sometimes these attempts go wrong – after the 1978 final, the then Leader of the Opposition Margaret Thatcher was asked for her man of the match. 'The Ipswich number ten, Trevor Whymark,' she replied. Unfortunately for Thatcher, who had seen his name in the programme, Whymark had been prevented from playing by injury.

- Everyone indulges in some misty-eyed nostalgia about the Cup Final anthem 'Abide With Me',

---

* Prince William might prove to be the exception to this rule, but then he supports Aston Villa which effectively proves the point.

despite knowing none of the words apart from the first three; 90,000 people join in with a rousing chorus of 'der, DER, der der-der-der'.

* For all the hype surrounding the build-up, the match itself is always awful. Both sets of players are so nervous that they can barely stand up, let alone do anything as complicated as kick a football.

* During the post-match celebrations, one of the victorious players takes the lid off the trophy and wears it as a hat. Nevertheless he still doesn't look as silly as he does wearing one of his designer suits.

Back in the days when absolutely every club (even the giants) took the FA Cup as seriously as possible, a number of 'classic' finals occurred. These have gone down in history, so you should know the basics:

1973, Sunderland 1 – Leeds United 0
Minnows Sunderland became the first second-tier team since 1931 to win the Cup. Leeds were then a huge side, and their defeat was all the more shocking because they were defending champions. The winning goal was scored by Ian Porterfield, who went on to achieve a unique place in football trivia: he was the first Premier League manager to be sacked (Chelsea, February 1993).

1976, Southampton 1 – Manchester United 0
Another victory by an unfancied Second Division team. The goal was scored by Bobby Stokes, not to be confused

with Bob Stokoe, manager of Sunderland in the 1973 final. These were the days when English football was peopled mostly by Englishmen.

1981, Tottenham Hotspur 3 – Manchester City 2

This match (the replay on the Thursday night following a 1–1 draw in the original match) is remembered for the final goal, a miraculous effort by Spurs' famously hirsute Argentinian player Ricky Villa (pronounced 'Vee-ah', not as in 'Aston…'). He dribbled the ball past what seemed like 37 City players in the penalty area before slotting it into the net. It's a frequent contender for 'Goal of the Century'.

1987, Coventry City 3 – Tottenham Hotspur 2

The mighty Spurs this time came off second best, owing to their defender Gary Mabbutt deflecting the ball into his own net to give unfashionable Coventry their winning goal. Supporters of the Midlands club responded by naming one of their fanzines *Gary Mabbutt's Knee*.

1988, Wimbledon 1 – Liverpool 0

More giant killing, this time spoiling Liverpool's plans for a League and Cup double. Dave Beasant made history by becoming the first goalkeeper to captain an FA Cup-winning side, and also the first one to save a penalty in the final (from Liverpool's John Aldridge). He later made less-welcome history by becoming the first player ever to put himself out of action for two months by dropping a jar of salad cream on his big toe.

The League Cup

Another knockout competition, but very much the Will Young to the FA Cup's Frank Sinatra. Unless, of course, your team is in with a chance of winning, when it suddenly becomes highly valued and respected. Its only other value is its capacity for confusing Americans who cannot understand that a 'knockout cup' has got the word 'league' in its title. This is just one of the many things they fail to understand about football (or 'Soccerball' as they have been known to call it). The tournament's sponsors since its inception in 1961 have included the pools company Littlewoods and the brewers Worthington and Carling (entirely appropriate for a sport whose players like gambling and drinking).

It is important to note that the competition has had many different names over the years, and was rebranded as the EFL Cup for the 2016/17 season (but confusingly known for sponsorship reasons as the Carabao Cup). Despite this most football supporters stubbornly insist on continuing to refer to it as the League Cup).

EUROPEAN CLUB COMPETITIONS

The Champions League

This is the competition in which the best teams from all over Europe compete against each other. The first section of the tournament is conducted on a league basis, after which it switches to a knockout cup format. Americans have been known to go into nervous convulsions when you try and explain this to them.

Despite the fact that it is called the Champions League, not every team in it is champion of their own country. The top three, and in some countries (such as England) even four, teams in the league go forward into the next season's Champions League. Thus it is possible to become champions of Europe while not actually champions of your own country. An example occurred in 2012 when Chelsea won the Champions League despite having finished sixth in the Premier League that season, and having qualified in the 2010/11 season by finishing as runners-up nine points behind Manchester United. (See how complicated football can be.)

In recent years, the Champions League has been a productive hunting ground for English clubs; from 2005 to 2012 every final except one included a side from England, and in 2008 both teams were from that country, Manchester United beating Chelsea on penalties. Since Celtic's famous victory over Inter Milan in 1967, other British holders of the trophy (previously known as the European Cup) have included Liverpool, Nottingham Forest, and Aston Villa. Not since the dying days of the Second World War have European capitals seen so many Brits asking where they can get a decent pint.

The Europa League
Previously known as the UEFA Cup, this is essentially the European equivalent of the League Cup. It was always a consolation trophy for the Continent's also-rans, and has recently become even more devalued by a format change in which teams 'drop' into the League when they're knocked out of the Champions League's

early stages. A bit like being eliminated from *The X Factor* and then being allowed to take part in the talent contest at Butlins Minehead. All of this cynicism about the Europa League persists, of course, until your own team does well in it, when it becomes the very definition of 'European glory'.

INTERNATIONAL COMPETITIONS

The World Cup

Held every four years, this is quite simply the biggest competition in world sport (with the possible exception of the Olympics). 32 footballing countries from around the globe, qualifying from regional groups, compete over a three-week period for the right to be crowned champions.

The initial stage is in a league format, with eight groups of four teams. All the countries within each group play each other once. After this stage has been completed, Scotland goes home.

The competition then operates on a straight knockout basis. As indeed do the England fans. There is a round with 16 teams in it (often known, with stunning originality, as 'the round of 16'), followed by the quarter-finals. After this stage has been completed, England normally goes home.

Only four European countries competed in the first World Cup, which was held in Uruguay in 1930. The others said they were reluctant to undertake the three-week boat journey to get to South America, so establishing the convention that in football it's always a good idea to get your excuses in early.

The tournament's most successful country is Brazil, which has lifted the trophy five times. In the run-up to the 2018 competition Germany were just one behind them on four (as indeed were Italy). Indeed most World Cup records see Brazil and Germany near or at the top – for instance just before the start of the 2018 tournament, the 'total number of matches played' saw Germany in the lead on 106, with Brazil just two behind them on 104. These statistics obviously change with each World Cup, so it is recommended that you show your bluffing credentials by wearily drawing attention to their ambiguity. For example Germany (at that point in history) topped both the table for most goals scored (224) and most goals conceded (121). This is hardly surprising in view of the number of extra games Germany have played.

Another cunning ploy is to keep some facts up your sleeve that won't be changing any time soon. For instance, the trophy itself, which replaced the original Jules Rimet trophy in 1974, is made of 18 carat gold and weighs over 6kg. It has space for 17 winners' names on the base, and with 10 already engraved on it the available space will not run out until the 2038 competition. Not that any of the winners get to keep it during their time as champions; they only get a gold-plated replica. The original stays with FIFA. One very unusual aspect of the 1950 World Cup in Brazil was that there wasn't a final. Not an official one, anyway. The winner was decided by the four group winners playing each other in a round-robin format to determine which was the champion. Uruguay emerged triumphant over Brazil in an unsurprisingly flat and unmemorable final game.

In 2006 the Swiss found themselves in the curious position of being knocked out despite not conceding a single goal in open play. They qualified from their group with three 'clean sheets' (footballing slang for a match in which your opponents don't score), then played Ukraine. After a 0–0 draw, they lost a penalty shoot-out.

The European Championship

Informally known as the 'Euros', and formerly known as the European Nations' Cup, this is the European equivalent of the World Cup and is also held every four years. Europhile politicians always celebrate it as an example of European integration and togetherness, ignoring the fact that its very essence is the individual European countries ferociously competing against each other, usually on wartime lines. This was self-evident in the very first European Championship, held in 1960. Spain boycotted the tournament in protest at the Soviet Union's involvement in the Spanish Civil War of the 1930s. The Soviet Union beat Yugoslavia 2–1 after extra time in Paris. They didn't like each other much, either.

It is now an official FIFA regulation that any commentary on a Brazil match must include the phrase 'samba-like' in relation to the skilful movement of one of their players.

TOTAL FOOTBALL

BRAZIL

For over half a century, the Brazilians have been the acknowledged masters of world football. A nation of street urchins kicking bundles of old rags around dusty back alleys will stand little chance against hyperinflation or political corruption, but they will certainly have an advantage on the football field.

The few Brazilians who can afford match tickets bring to the terraces a carnival atmosphere that is second to none. It is now an official FIFA regulation that any commentary on a Brazil match must include the phrase 'samba-like' in relation to the skilful movement of one of their players.

The Brazilian side that won the 1970 World Cup and contained such greats as Pelé, Jairzinho, Rivelino and Gerson is reckoned by many to be the greatest team ever to step on to a football pitch. In the 1990s the torch of Brazilian genius passed to Ronaldo, notable as the only centre forward ever whose name sounded as though he should be an entertainer on the northern working men's club circuit. In more recent times the country's fans have worshipped Neymar Jr (full name Neymar da Silva Santos Junior, usually referred to simply as 'Neymar'), who in 2017 became the most expensive player ever by moving from Barcelona to Paris St Germain for 222 million Euros. This astonishing figure has been cited as evidence of football's increasing detachment not just from the average fan but from reality. But it is recommended that bluffers cite Neymar as a model of good behaviour, except when he is timed spending more than 14 minutes feigning injury on the pitch. A committed Christian, he has been rumoured to donate 10% of his income to the church. And when his son was born, he described the new arrival as '2.8 kilograms of pure happiness'. This phrase would have had a very different meaning for one particular player from Brazil's rivals Argentina, the football genius and former cocaine addict Diego Maradona. The ultimate acknowledgement of this nation's footballing prowess is the chant heard regularly on English terraces when a team is playing well. It is sung to the tune of 'Blue Moon': 'Brazil, it's just like watching Brazil, it's just like…' Chelsea fans, on the other hand, in the distant days when their team was utterly inept, would chant: '*The Bill*, it's just like watching *The Bill*, it's just like…'

FRANCE

For many years France had a self-defeating attitude to football and the temperamental nature of their star players often jeopardised the national team's chances of success. Eric Cantona, for instance, hailed as a god in his club football for Manchester United, fell out with the French manager, thereby depriving the team of a crucial player. And David Ginola, who made a mistake in a qualifying game that prevented France from reaching the 1994 World Cup Finals, was publicly rebuked for it by the then national manager Gérard Houllier. With typical French restraint, Houllier called the error a 'crime' (or perhaps he was referring to Ginola's latest advert for shampoo/aftershave/underwear). All was bitterness and underachievement, which for English fans was a beautiful and satisfying spectacle.

But then, in the late 1990s, France inexplicably shrugged off their internecine squabbling and started to win tournaments. Enormously talented players like Zinedine Zidane, Marcel Desailly and Emmanuel Petit melded into a formidable side that won the 1998 World Cup, then the 2000 European Championship, and then the 2018 World Cup with one of the youngest squads in the competition (which doesn't bode well for the future prospects of rival teams). The success of French football is a profoundly disturbing phenomenon with which England fans have still not come to terms.

GERMANY

For many years the German football team dominated Europe in a way that their military leaders never quite got the hang of. World Cup winners in 1954, 1974, 1990 and 2014, and European champions in 1972, 1980 and 1996, their style of football was, unsurprisingly, a very efficient one. Especially infuriating was the fact that somewhere along the line their victories usually involved beating England in a penalty shoot-out. But when players of the mental robustness of Michael Ballack and Lothar Matthäus step forward to take a penalty, not even the most deluded England optimists imagine for a moment that there's any chance of them missing.

Despite this, the English fans continue to taunt their Teutonic rivals with the time-honoured chant (to the tune of 'Camptown Races'), 'Two World Wars and one World Cup, doo-dah, doo-dah…' The only reason that the Germans don't chant back is that 'Four World Cups, three European Championships and a vastly superior economic infrastructure established after our nation's humiliating defeat in 1945' hasn't got much of a ring to it.

ITALY

The joint-second most successful team in World Cup history, Italy's tally of four titles (1934, 1938, 1982, 2006) puts them only one behind Brazil. Therefore their failure to qualify for the 2018 tournament was a shock to football fans the world over: a World Cup without Italy is like a pizza without tomato sauce. Anyone who doubts that Italy is a nation of opera lovers should watch one of its footballers appealing for a penalty. The passion and torment etched agonisingly into his face, his arms gesticulating madly as he beseeches the referee in vain, the unbearable sense of injustice that sends him crashing to the ground, a broken and defeated man –

an Italian centre forward can inject a simple handball decision with the sort of drama normally only seen on the stage of La Scala. While all this melodrama is going on up front, the defenders, historically led by the likes of Paolo Maldini and Fabio Cannavaro, are busy building an impregnable wall capable of comfortably repelling Attila the Hun and his invading hordes.

Anyone who doubts that Italy is a nation of opera lovers should watch one of its footballers appealing for a penalty.

ARGENTINA

Argentina rivals Germany and Scotland as England's most bitter rival in international football. Much of this ill-feeling dates from Maradona's 'hand of God' incident in the 1986 World Cup (*see* 'Great Players' page 78), but the enmity was there even before this. In the first round knock-out stage of the 1966 World Cup, England manager Alf Ramsey was reported to have described Argentina's players as 'animals' for being somewhat over-competitive, and refused to allow England players to swap shirts with their opponents at the end of the match. This didn't go down well in Argentina. Then, in 1982, the two countries went to war over the Falkland Islands, making things very difficult for the two Argentinian players then at Tottenham Hotspur, Ricky Villa and Ossie Ardiles. So fierce was the feeling that

Ardiles preferred to spend six months on loan to French club Paris Saint-Germain.

Diego Maradona has recently been challenged for the title of 'best player ever' (not just in Argentina – but in the world) by fellow Argentinian Lionel Messi. (*See* 'Great Players' page 79.) A genius he may be, but Messi proved more than a little petulant when Argentina lost the 2016 Copa America (South America's equivalent of the European Championship) to Chile. He was annoyed that he had never won a major trophy with his country – after all, his club career at Barcelona has featured more trophies than you could shake a feather duster at. So he did what any hard-working, conscientious professional sportsman would do: he announced he wasn't going to play ball any more. Two years previously he had lost in the World Cup final, and it simply wasn't fair to expect him to carry on playing for his country if the results were always going to go against him (to paraphrase slightly). Thankfully for Argentina's fans – and indeed for the rest of the world, who realise just how great Messi is, the temperamental striker reversed his decision just two months later.

You can point out that Argentinian footballers are never too far from controversy. In 2006 Leandro Cufré became the only player ever sent off after the final whistle of a World Cup game, when Argentina and Germany had a mass fight following their quarter-final. What made Cufré's achievement even more incredible is that he was a substitute, and hadn't even taken part in the game. Yes, you can be sent off without having come on first. This is one of the illogicalities that makes football the sport that it is.

THE NETHERLANDS

Always a strong side, the Dutch have over the years given us such exquisitely gifted players as Johan Cruyff, Marco van Basten, Ruud Gullit and Dennis Bergkamp. But for English fans, the most significant Dutch player ever was Ronald Koeman. In a qualifying match for the 1994 World Cup, he scored against England when he shouldn't even have been on the pitch (the referee having failed to send him off for an earlier foul on David Platt). As a result, England did not make it to the Finals. As a consequence of that, the late Graham Taylor was forced to resign as national manager. As much as Taylor subsequently earned a place in the nation's heart for his commentary work and club management style, his England sacking was a service for which Koeman won the eternal gratitude of English fans.

SPAIN

Rather like France, Spain were for many years perennial underachievers. All that changed, however, when they won the 2008 and 2012 European Championships ('Euros'), slotting the 2010 World Cup in between them to make a very tasty *bocadillo* of victories. (Indeed it was the first time any team had ever completed such a hat-trick.) Spain's domestic sides have always been among the very best in Europe, and it has come as no surprise that the national team is now recognised as one of the best of all time. Furious at their ability to win the 2012 Euros without the use of a recognised centre forward (although they brought on the hapless Fernando Torres every now and then), critics in the English tabloid press derided their reliance on 'passing too much', otherwise known as 'keeping the ball'. This is something akin to cheating in English eyes, and there is little appreciation of the likes of Xavi, Iniesta and Silva dancing around their opponents and scoring whenever they feel like it.

USA

'Football' is one of those words that Americans just do not understand (like 'pavement', 'nappy', 'fanny' and 'irony'). To them, football is a game in which men weighing 18 stone put on protective clothing weighing 19 stone and throw a rugby-shaped ball around a field with more lines on it than an Ordnance Survey map.

What we call football is known in the USA as 'soccer'. The game should never be referred to as such. Anyone using this unacceptable term will instantly be suspected of demonstrating the same naivety about the game that Americans do. But if you ever want to display a 'next level up' degree of bluffmanship, allow those around you to smirk at the 's' word for a while, then remind them that we shouldn't, after all, blame it on the Americans themselves. It derives from the 'soc' in 'Association', the word that distinguishes football from rugby (see 'Rules of engagement' page 9). You yourself would never call the game 'soccer', your friends should understand – but equally you wouldn't want to blame its introduction on the Americans. No need: there are more than enough other things to blame them for.

Popularity of the sport in the States has been led by the success of the country's women's team, which won the 1999 World Cup by beating China in the final (Americans always like beating another superpower). But the USA's lack of a feel for the game was perhaps best displayed by the 1970s coach of the New York Cosmos, who had signed the German Franz Beckenbauer, famously the most gifted defender of his era. 'Tell the Kraut to get his ass up front,' he famously said. 'We don't pay a million for a guy to hang around in defence.' Successful US players tend to be independent mavericks who find their way to England's Premier League and kick some serious butt. Examples include Tottenham Hotspur's shaven-headed midfield dynamo Clint Dempsey. But shaven-headed Yanks also make remarkably good goalkeepers, including Brad Friedel (also Spurs), Tim Howard (Everton) and Marcus Hahnemann (formerly of Reading).

REPUBLIC OF IRELAND

Desperate for international success, the country has relaxed its qualification criteria to the point that you can now play for Ireland as long as at least one of your grandparents once drank a pint of Guinness. One of their greatest-ever players was Roy Keane, who spent most of his time berating his fellow Irishmen, especially if they had been born in England. But score serious bluffing points for mentioning that Johnny Giles consistently tops all-time great Irish player rankings. Legendary Manchester United manager Sir Matt Busby described his decision to let Giles leave United to join Leeds in 1963 as his 'greatest ever mistake in football'. Giles went on to personify the concept of 'player-manager' at West Bromwich Albion in 1975, and filled the team with Irish players. Unsurprisingly, it became known as West Bromwich Éirann.

SCOTLAND

For many years, the story of the Scottish Premier League was the same every season. There were ten teams: Glasgow Rangers, Glasgow Celtic and the eight other clubs who those two played to decide which of them would win the title that year. Then, in 2012, the financial madness that has gripped Scottish (and indeed English) football in recent years came knocking on the door. When Rangers opened that door they found Her Majesty's Revenue and Customs demanding £9 million in unpaid tax. Behind the HMRC stood several midfields' worth of other creditors, and behind them stood the Premier League saying, 'Righto, you know the rules about clubs' financial health.' Those rules meant, in a deep-fried nutshell, that Rangers were chucked out of the league and demoted to the Third Division. The same logic – i.e., a complete lack of it – applies in Scotland as in England, meaning that the Third Division is in fact the fourth division. There are falls from grace, and then there are plummets into a chasm of gracelessness so deep that the footballing world shakes on its axis.

In terms of international football, Scotland fulfils a key role. They consistently do even worse than England in World Cups, which ensures that the English fans have got at least something to laugh about.

ENGLAND

NB: this entry is far longer than that of other more successful nations for one very simple reason: the English invented football. As a cogent argument, this holds less water than George Best took with his Scotch, but no matter; pig-headed, self-deluding self-importance is a vital component of the English footballing mentality, and as a skilled bluffer you should be aware of that.

There are many great moments in the history of the England football team. Unfortunately from an English point of view, they all occurred on 30 July 1966.

The basic story of England's triumph in the World Cup Final at Wembley is simple. With minutes to go, they lead 2–1. But tragedy strikes when Wolfgang Weber equalises for the West Germans. England fans are as 'sick as parrots' (*see* 'Glossary'). In the first period of extra time, Geoff Hurst strikes a shot that rebounds off the underside of the crossbar, hits the ground and bounces back out of the goal. The Russian (actually Azerbaijanian, but in 1966 'Soviet' and 'Russian' were used interchangeably, certainly by people at the 'football fan' level of geo-cultural awareness) linesman Tofiq Bakhramov controversially decides that the ball crossed the line, and England therefore take the lead (not the first time that England and Russia have combined to defeat the Germans). In the dying seconds of the game, Hurst scores another goal, becoming the only player ever to score a hat-trick in a World Cup Final. 'Some people are on the pitch, they think it's all over. It is now!' was Kenneth Wolstenholme's famous commentary.

So well worn is this story that in order to gain any respect from fellow fans, you need to be armed with a couple of little-known facts about the match:

- The England players' match fee was a mere £60 each. Adidas offered £1,000 to any player who agreed to wear the company's boots for the final – several did, while others painted three white stripes on the side of their existing boots to make them *look* like Adidas (the firm also paid the £1,000 for this).

- If the scores had still been level at the end of extra time, there would have been a replay. If that failed to settle the matter, the World Cup would have been decided not by another replay, not by a penalty shoot-out – but by the toss of a coin.

- When Hurst scored the fourth goal, one of the English trainers was so excited he jumped up in wild celebration. The notoriously dour and strait-laced England manager Alf Ramsey told him: 'Sit down and behave yourself.'

England have never again reached the final of a major competition. But there have been some near misses and you should always have several up your sleeve. For instance:

1970, Mexico, World Cup quarter-final v West Germany

Having led 2–0, England somehow manage to lose the

match 3–2. Many blame the last-minute replacement goalkeeper Peter Bonetti. His usual nickname was 'The Cat', on account of his incredible agility. That day he gets called one or two other names. Also, substitute centre forward Jeff Astle misses an absolute sitter from about 18 inches. Shortly afterwards he takes up a new career as a window cleaner.

1990, Italy, World Cup semi-final v West Germany

The score at the end of extra time is 1–1. The match goes to a penalty shoot-out. Stuart Pearce having missed, Chris Waddle must score to keep England in the tournament. His shot seriously endangers the man sitting in row P, seat 184.

Over the following years, Phil Collins earns substantial royalties from his song 'I Missed Again' being played over the footage of Pearce and Waddle's penalties.

1996, Wembley, European Championship semi-final v Germany

Again the match goes to penalties. Both sides score all of their first five penalties. Gareth Southgate steps up to take England's sixth.

Phil Collins orders a new car.

1998, France, World Cup v Argentina

Despite David Beckham's sending off, England's ten men manage to take the match to a penalty shoot-out. Paul Ince misses. David Batty must score to prevent England going out of the tournament.

Phil Collins goes to live in Switzerland.

In recent tournaments England have developed a not-very-enviable reputation for losing in the last eight, exiting at that stage in the 2002 and 2006 World Cups, as well as the 2004 and 2012 European Championships. Not so much a case of no quarter given as no quarter-final won. Many fans have come to expect nothing more of England. The disillusionment is all the greater because high-profile foreign managers (Sven-Göran Eriksson, Fabio Capello) secured enormous salaries on the promise of delivering success, then delivered just more failure. The middle bit of Eriksson's name, incidentally, is pronounced 'urine'. Appropriate, as this is what a lot of people thought he was taking.

An all-time low in the nation's football fortunes came in the 2016 Euros when the national team suffered one of the greatest humiliations in its history when plucky little Iceland came from behind to defeat England 1-2 in the last 16, prompting the immediate resignation of manager Roy Hodgson. Iceland has a population roughly the size of Coventry.

But then, redemption! England learned to love its football team again in the 2018 World Cup when it finished a creditable fourth after defeat in the semi finals by Croatia, a country with a population roughly half the size of London. After three weeks of deluded fans singing 'Football's Coming Home', England's predictable exit reasserted a sense of normality – even if the mood was more heroic failure than the customary abject capitulation. Sadly football wasn't coming home, it was doing something much worse – it was coming uncomfortably close to home instead, just 18 nautical miles across the English Channel.

ENGLISH TEAMS

MANCHESTER UNITED

Manchester United is an international leisure, clothing and merchandising conglomerate, worth hundreds of millions of pounds, and with interests in every major country around the world. As a sideline, it also runs a football team.

All you need to know about this football team is summed up in the statement that there are only three clubs whose names contain a swear word – Arsenal, Scunthorpe and F***ing Man United. The team completely dominated English football during the 1990s, and even though other sides have come to challenge that dominance in recent years, Man U (as they are known) are still widely disliked by other fans. This is in large part due to the lofty attitude displayed by their long-time Scottish manager Sir Alex Ferguson, now retired. The Man United management is often accused of being paranoid. This is unfair. Paranoia is the state of falsely perceiving that everyone hates you. Man U are perfectly correct in their perception that everyone hates them.

There are only three clubs whose names contain a swear word – Arsenal, Scunthorpe and F***ing Man United.

If, as an advanced bluffer, you wish to argue against the prevailing 'United Are Evil' thesis, there are a couple of facts to which you could refer:

• Man U won all their trophies during Ferguson's time playing dynamic and entertaining football, as opposed to the safe but dull defensive style favoured by some other teams.

• The club's worldwide appeal was a major factor in attracting attention to the Premier League, thereby making it an appealing place for the globe's best players to come and ply their trade, so giving British football fans great entertainment.

The alternative is simply to hate them like everyone else. It's easier.

MANCHESTER CITY

This is the team supported by everyone who lives in Manchester. As opposed to Manchester United, which is the team supported by everyone who lives in Surrey. For years City played Watson to United's Holmes (in fact, even that's not right – Holmes and Watson liked each other), but the injection in 2008 of massive funding by new owners the Abu Dhabi United Group (run by a member of that country's Royal family) changed the picture completely. Since then, Man City (as they are known) have qualified for the Champions League and won the FA Cup (2011) and Premier League (2012, 2014, and 2018). Their fans' celebrations have been only slightly dimmed by the fact that the organisation responsible for all this success has the word 'United' in its name.

All this is a long way from the dark days of the mid-1990s, when City even slipped down to the third tier of English football. The club was in such a mess that at one point they had 42 players on the books. Manager Alan Ball said that as they ran towards him on his first day in charge he felt like Michael Caine in *Zulu*.

CHELSEA

A successful team, runs the old footballing cliché, requires a 'blend of youth and experience'. Chelsea's capture of the 2005, 2006, 2010, 2015 and 2017 Premier League titles, the 2007, 2009, 2010 and 2012 FA Cups, the 2012 Champions League and the 2013 Europa League proved that, as with Manchester City, nowadays it's a blend of half a billion pounds and another half a billion pounds. The Blues' purchase by Russian oil zillionaire Roman Abramovich has given the team its new nickname: 'Chelski'. The club was already famous for buying expensive overseas players. It has now imported so many that it is rumoured to have its own customs channel at Heathrow airport.

(Make sure to mention that this trend is the opposite of that which occurred during the 1980s, when many of the best English footballers went to play on the Continent. By and large these moves turned out to be failures. It is often thought that this was because the players didn't speak the languages of the countries they'd moved to. But this belief is a mistaken one; after all, not being able to speak English had never stopped them getting on at home. Rather, the problem lay in the fact that the players missed their traditional English food, such as curries, kebabs and chicken chow mein.)

Although his money has brought Chelsea huge success, Abramovich has become known for his impatience with underachieving managers. After promptly dismissing the incumbent team boss Claudio 'The Tinkerman' Ranieri, and then losing José Mourinho (who achieved the Roman Emperor's first bout of consecutive successes), several other foreign bosses such as Avram Grant, Luiz Felipe Scolari and André Villas-Boas have come and gone. Not even winning the FA Cup and the Champions League in the same season (2012), as achieved by Roberto Di Matteo, is any guarantee of job security. To underline just how temporary any manager's position is at Stamford Bridge (the club's West London ground), note what happened when the deeply unpopular former Liverpool manager Rafa Benítez was sacked in 2013. His replacement was José Mourinho, back for a second spell at 'the Bridge' after his triumphs of 2004–7. He won Chelsea the Premiership in 2015 – then was sacked for a second time after an abysmal start to the next season.

ARSENAL

One of the two main north London clubs. Although in recent years the other one, Tottenham Hotspur, have enjoyed a resurgence in form, they still haven't actually won the top-flight title (old First Division or Premier League) since 1961. Arsenal have won it several times, and indeed in 1998 and 2002 they did the 'double' (winning both the league and the FA Cup in the same season). This annoys Spurs fans immensely, especially as Arsenal aren't even proper north Londoners; they were originally from Woolwich in south London. The club crossed the river in 1913, but even today Tottenham fans still give their rivals the very keenest encouragement to make the return journey.

In 1996 they appointed as manager the lugubrious Frenchman Arsène Wenger, who became notorious for his bad eyesight when asked to comment on any suggestion that his team might be at fault in some respect. Remarkably, that vision became keener than a hawk's when there was any suggestion his team might have been offended against. His 22 years in charge made him the club's longest-serving manager. Arsenal's old stadium, Highbury, was renowned for its immaculate pitch. Until the mid-1990s the team was also known for its grindingly dull defensive tactics, to the extent that it was often more interesting to watch the famous grass grow than it was to concentrate on the play. In its latter years the ground was nicknamed 'Highbury the Library', on account of the team's middle-class fans clapping politely instead of roaring on their team. It was once worked out that the energy of 10,000 football fans cheering is sufficient to boil three pints of water. At an Arsenal match you might just get enough for a teaspoon.

TOTTENHAM HOTSPUR

As noted previously, it has been a while since Spurs won the league. They traditionally performed more strongly in cups than in the league. Their claim that they always win the FA Cup 'when the year ends in one' is based on the fact that they won the competition in 1961, 1981 and 1991. They tend to shut up about the theory when you point out to them that the 1971 winners were their hated rivals Arsenal, and that they were conspicuous by their absence in 2001 and 2011. No matter. They can always look forward to 2021.

A piece of linguistic trivia to throw in whenever Spurs are mentioned is that the club's name is the only one of the top 92 teams to end in 'r'. (People assume from the common abbreviation that the club's full name is 'Tottenham Hotspurs' – not so.)

LIVERPOOL

Under legendary managers Bill Shankly and Bob Paisley, and with players of the class of Kevin Keegan, Kenny Dalglish and Ian Rush, Liverpool were the most successful English club from the 1960s until the 1980s. Countless League trophies, FA Cups, League Cups and European Cups (the old name for the Champions League) made their way to the trophy cabinet at the club's ground.

Since 1990, and despite the presence of many

immensely talented players such as Michael Owen and Steven Gerrard, Liverpool have failed to win the top-flight title. They won the FA Cup in 2001 and 2006, and even managed to (as many people saw it) 'fluke' the Champions League in 2005 (they came from 3–0 down at half-time in the final to win on penalties) – but until the 'Reds' win the Premier League their fans will feel short-changed.

In the meantime, though, those supporters continue to support the side vigorously. They're famous for the anthem 'You'll Never Walk Alone'. Opposition fans frequently change this to 'You'll Never Work Again' (including the refrain, 'Sign on, sign on, with a pen in your hand…').

EVERTON

The other team in Liverpool, and perennial under-achievers. Their ground, Goodison Park, is adjacent to a church which actually protrudes into the ground – but not actually on to the pitch. The club does not play early kick-offs on Sundays in order to permit Sunday services at the church to proceed uninterrupted. However, even having God as a season ticket holder hasn't helped them match the historic success achieved by Liverpool.

NEWCASTLE UNITED

Known as the 'Magpies', their fans are renowned both for their unwavering loyalty and for their hardiness. On the very coldest of winter days, they occasionally relent and wear a second T-shirt.

The typical footballer of the 1950s smoked 30 cigarettes a day, drank 8 pints of bitter a night, and his average evening meal contained only slightly less grease than the engine of his second-hand Morris Minor.

THEN AND NOW

THEN

The typical English footballer of the 1950s was born and raised in a tough coal-mining area. He turned to the sport only after failing to get accepted for a job down the pit which provided better pay and working conditions than football.

He addressed the manager of his club as 'sir', and even that only when he was spoken to first. He cleaned his own boots, which weighed approximately a third of a stone each. His wages were £15 a week (£12 in the summer) – the maximum wage of £20 a week was not abolished by the Football Association until 1961.

The typical footballer smoked 30 cigarettes a day, drank 8 pints of bitter a night, and his average evening meal contained only slightly less grease than the engine of his second-hand Morris Minor. His team's matches were always on a Saturday afternoon or a Wednesday night (and even that only became common after floodlights were introduced). He shared a bath with ten other players, and washed his hair with carbolic soap.

After his retirement from the game he ran a pub, or – if he had been particularly successful – two pubs.

NOW

The typical footballer of today is signed by his first club at the age of 14, upon which his assistant agent (contracts) negotiates his first endorsement deal with a leisurewear manufacturer. He then progresses through the youth and reserve teams, making his Premier League debut two weeks before he takes delivery of his first Ferrari, and four weeks before he can legally start learning to drive his first Ferrari.

Having turned in a series of adequate performances, he is billed by his agent as 'the next Messi', which leads several other clubs to bid increasingly obscene amounts for his signature. He is eventually transferred for an eight-figure sum to a club who pay him more in a week than his parents earn together in a year.

His games are sometimes on a Saturday afternoon, but often on almost any other day of the week, depending on whether Sky have switched the match to Sunday afternoon or Monday evening to suit their TV schedule, or how long the other team have been allowed to recover from their quarter-final, second-leg Europa League tie the previous Thursday in the Ukraine.

His girlfriend is a pop star, or a model, or a pop star who used to be a model. She is blonde.

He cannot understand why you would want to go abroad, unless it's to get a suntan. This attitude was best illustrated by the West Bromwich Albion player John Trewick who, on a tour of China, was offered the chance to see the Great Wall. He declined, saying that 'Once you've seen one wall, you've seen them all.'

After today's typical footballer retires from the game, he will play golf.

Graeme Souness played for Liverpool and was renowned for his uncompromising tackling. (That's 'uncompromising' in the sense that Mount Kilimanjaro is 'a bit of a climb'.)

GREAT PLAYERS

'Who-was-the-greatest-player-ever?' debates have for years ended up with two names competing for the winning vote:

PELÉ

This Brazilian legend scored 1,281 goals in a career that redefined footballing greatness. From his initial appearance in the 1958 World Cup, where at the age of 17 he scored two of the goals that won Brazil the final, to his retirement in 1977, he was acknowledged as the most astoundingly skilful player in the world – especially by himself. There is not much point in disputing his talent.

Far greater value is to be gained by learning Pelé's real name: Edson Arantes do Nascimento. Useful for showing off, but be careful not to do it with your mouth full. Pelé has always claimed that he has never understood the provenance of his nickname, although popular belief has it that it is the Portuguese word for 'pearl'. In fact 'pele' means 'skin' in Portuguese.

DIEGO MARADONA

Argentinian star whose breathtaking skills on the ball confounded entire defences, but whom England fans will forever associate with England's exit from the 1986 World Cup. Advancing one-on-one against the England goalkeeper Peter Shilton to meet a high ball with his head, Maradona instead raised his arm to punch the ball into the net. This was blatantly obvious to Shilton, to the other players, to the crowd in the stadium, and to millions of TV viewers around the world. Unfortunately there was one person to whom it was not obvious – the referee, Ali Bin Nasser of Tunisia. He gave the goal, Argentina won the match 2–1, and England were out of the tournament. Even Maradona himself went halfway to admitting he had cheated, cynically claiming that the goal had been scored 'with the hand of God'. Coincidentally, England fans to this day still respond to any mention of Diego Maradona with a gesture in which the hand also features quite heavily.

OTHER NAMES

In the second decade of the 21st century, Pelé and Maradona finally attracted some competition for the title of 'greatest player ever'. The two new names in the frame were the players who for several years traded the Ballon d'Or (the annual award for the world's best male player) between them: Lionel Messi (of Barcelona and Argentina) and Cristiano Ronaldo (of Juventus and Portugal). Ronaldo's skill is impossible to deny, but few serious fans would call him the best player ever. As he progressed into his thirties he tended to restrict his contributions to occasional touches of the ball in the penalty area – yes they were astonishing, and yes they often produced goals, but you couldn't call them a *constant* display of terrifying genius.

DO SAY: 'Did you know that Ronaldo was named after Ronald Reagan?' Instead of getting sidetracked into assessing Ronaldo's ranking in the all-time list, earn yourself some points by revealing this little-known fact. In Portugal the first two names are given – his full name is Cristiano Ronaldo dos Santos Aveiro. This wasn't a political statement, although coincidentally Reagan was US President when the player was born in 1985 – rather it was because Ronaldo's father was a fan of Reagan's movies.

DON'T SAY: 'Did you know that Lionel Messi was named after Lionel Richie?' This 'fact' did the rounds after it became known that Ronaldo was named after Reagan – sadly it's an urban myth.

The real contender for the 'greatest ever' crown is Lionel Messi. Some commentators have already made the call – for instance during Barcelona's Champions League win over Chelsea in March 2018 the ex-England player Alan Shearer tweeted: 'We should consider ourselves very fortunate to live in an era where we can watch the greatest player ever! #Messi'

Even those who still argue for Pelé or Maradona

might, in time, come to change their minds. Messi's ball skills are utterly extraordinary – it was once said that he could 'nutmeg a mermaid'. (*See* 'Glossary'.) The look of terror on defenders' faces as the Argentinian dribbles the ball towards them tells you everything – it's not just that they know he's going to go round them, it's that they're going to end up looking stupid into the bargain. They could very well be watching him smash the ball into the net from a seated position, having fallen over trying to cope with his final twist of the body.

BLUFFER'S TIP *Instead of trying to out-superlative your colleagues about Messi, wait for their praise to die down then utter the simple phrase: 'Tidy player, Messi.' If there's anything football fans love more than sublime play it's atrocious puns. While we're on the subject of names, Messi's first is sometimes pronounced 'Lee-oh-nell'. This may be the Argentinian way of saying it, but if anyone pulls you up for pronouncing 'Lionel' as in 'Blair', simply point out that we don't talk about going to 'Pah-ree' for the weekend.*

Great as Messi is, you could stand out from the crowd by throwing some alternative names into the mix. There's **Zinedine Zidane**, the Frenchman who helped his country win the 1998 World Cup and 2000 European Championship. He has always been a favourite with football purists, as much for his temper as his silky skills. It was fitting, if a touch sad, that in the final match of his career, the 2006 World Cup Final, he was sent off for headbutting an opponent in the chest. Earn some extra bluffing points for demolishing an urban myth that has grown up about Zidane since his retirement, namely that he went his entire career without ever being caught offside. In fact this is untrue; he was caught offside at least four times. This is still an incredibly low figure for an attacking midfielder – but your awareness of the truth will mark you out as a fully paid member of the footballing cognoscenti.

Another good choice is **Johan Cruyff,** whose deftness and poise on the ball entertained millions during his time in the great Holland side of the 1970s, as well as a club career that included winning three successive European Cups with Ajax. Highlight the fact that he achieved his incredible feats of athleticism despite being a heavy smoker. That sort of thing appeals to football fans. (A more recent smoker was Chelsea's Gianluca Vialli. Fans also loved him for his linguistic slip-ups, though many of these were tricks played on him by his players when he took over as manager – most notably his claim that you have to work hard 'when the fish are down'.)

A safe choice for the greatest defender ever is **Franz Beckenbauer.** He became famous as the first player to see the attacking possibilities of this role; having successfully prevented a goal, he would quickly push forward and split open the opposition with a single, perfectly placed pass, thereby allowing his own side to score. You can feel confident about commending him to English fans even though he's German. Yes, he really was that good.

GREAT DOMESTIC PLAYERS

Sir Stanley Matthews

Mercurial midfielder whose dazzling skills earned him the nickname 'the Wizard of Dribble'. Dribbling is what pundits tend to do when they eulogise about his performance in the 1953 FA Cup Final, when he consistently outfoxed his Bolton Wanderers opponents. What they never mention is that Blackpool won the match thanks to a Stan Mortensen hat-trick; Matthews didn't score a single goal. Bluffers will need to know that he was still playing first team football for Stoke at the age of 50.

Sir Bobby Charlton

Played in England's World Cup-winning side of 1966. Had scored more goals for England (49) and Manchester United (249) than anyone else until Wayne Rooney broke both records. Many of these were aided by the fact that the opposing defenders were too busy being distracted by his hairstyle (a magnificent comb-over) to concentrate on the ball.

Bobby Moore

As the only England captain ever to lift the World Cup, Moore would have been guaranteed a place in fans' hearts anyway. That bond was cemented by the fact that Moore was a supremely gifted player (Pelé called him the best defender he ever played against) and a charming, charismatic bloke to boot. His death from cancer at the age of only 51 saddened the whole country.

Whenever his name is mentioned people emit a fond, reverent sigh – you should join in, then score some bluffing points by revealing that one of Moore's middle names was Chelsea. Nothing to do with the club – he was a West Ham player for most of his career – it was just a given name often used in the Moore family.

Bryan Robson

His leadership of Manchester United and England earned him the nickname 'Captain Marvel'. In 1982 he scored what was at the time thought to be the fastest-ever goal in the history of the World Cup finals – 27 seconds. (Subsequent checks found that in 1962 Czechoslovakia's Vaclav Masek had scored in 15 seconds. The record is now held by Turkey's Hakan Sukur, whose 2002 goal took just 11 seconds.)

Sir Kenny Dalglish

Played for Celtic and Liverpool in the 1970s and 1980s, building a knowledge of the game that is second to none. Unfortunately his totally incomprehensible Scottish accent means that he can't pass any of it on. This linguistic handicap was also probably one of the reasons for his summary dismissal as manager by Liverpool's American owners at the end of the 2011/12 season.

Gary Lineker

One of the most prolific goalscorers of the modern era. Never booked or sent off (largely because his permanent position – two feet out from the goal line – meant he was rarely close enough to the play to foul anyone).

Graeme Souness

Played for Liverpool and was renowned for his uncompromising tackling. (That's 'uncompromising' in the sense that Mount Kilimanjaro is 'a bit of a climb'.)

Glenn Hoddle

Spurs and England midfielder cited by many as the most naturally gifted player of his generation. Affectionately known as 'Glenda', he became England manager before being sacked for comments concerning reincarnation (and some other weird stuff involving clairvoyants). His name subsequently became student rhyming slang for 'doddle'.

Paul Gascoigne

At the beginning of his career, discussions about Gazza usually contained the words 'genius', 'gifted' and 'sublime'. It's important – if tragically ironic – to remember that.

George Best

As a teenage prodigy from Belfast, Best signed with Manchester United in 1963, and went on to win both the First Division and the European Cup with them. His skills on the ball were legendary; so was his drinking. As for his off-the-field activities, bluffers should remember Best's famous remark: 'I spent 90% of my money on drink, women and fast cars. The rest I wasted.'

Michael Owen

First shot to attention at the 1998 World Cup, when a wonder goal against Argentina made him the youngest player ever to score for England (he was 18 – it wasn't until 2003 that the record was broken, by Wayne Rooney). Unfortunately his early promise was never completely fulfilled. Playing most of his career at Liverpool meant he was doomed never to win the Premier League. Playing for England meant he was doomed never to win a major trophy. Rarely are multimillionaires described as 'doomed' – but football fans like to dwell on negatives.

Ryan Giggs

His longevity in Manchester United's first team brought him the unusual achievement of being the only player to score in each of the first 21 seasons of the Premier League's history (and the only player to appear in each of the first 22 seasons). A Twitter naming campaign brought him the less enviable achievement of having his alleged extra-marital scoring record plastered all over the Internet – the same Internet that had barely existed when he made his United debut in 1991.

Frank Lampard

A firm favourite with fans of his long-term club Chelsea, Lampard is a useful card to play when it comes to the 'Are there any intelligent footballers?' discussion. Not only does his reported IQ of over 150 qualify him for Mensa, he also achieved 11 GCSEs, including an A* in Latin.

Wayne Rooney

The Manchester United and England star went a long way after his first appearance on a Premier League pitch;

as a spud-faced nipper of 11 he was the mascot for his beloved Everton when they played Liverpool during the 1996/97 season. Rooney is an equally useful card to play when it comes to the 'Are there any intelligent footballers?' discussion. But only if your answer is, 'No'.

Steven Gerrard

The Liverpool midfielder and England captain was unusual for sharing with Ryan Giggs the rare distinction of having only played for one club. In 2015 he left Anfield to play for a season with the American side LA Galaxy, doing little to dispel the widely held view that US soccer clubs are little more than retirement homes for ageing UK players. In 2009 Zinedine Zidane said of Gerrard that he was the best player in the world. To date he is the only footballer to have scored a goal in both domestic cup competitions, a UEFA Cup final, and a Champions League final.

David Beckham

What is there left to say about the lachrymose multi-tattooed midfield dynamo and darling of the England football establishment? Only one thing: 'Arise Sir David.' And that might take a while, after Beckham's expletive-packed reaction to being overlooked for a knighthood in 2013 because of questions about his tax arrangements. (The expletives only came to light because of hacked emails, but Beckham is said to have accepted that the big gong might have ridden over the horizon for now.) In the meantime the man widely known as 'Goldenballs' will continue to represent England and the UK at all major sporting events, hobnob with royalty and political leaders, and show off his impressively packed underpants on advertising hoardings around the world. In footballing terms, he is the third most capped England player, with 115 appearances (behind only Peter Shilton and Wayne Rooney), and he was famously described as having a right foot 'like a scalpel'. By all accounts he's also a jolly good chap, and no one should begrudge him his estimated £165 million fortune. Not at all.

Gareth Bale

The unassuming Welsh winger transferred from Tottenham Hotspur to Real Madrid in 2013 for a then record fee of 100 million Euros. Among many notable career highlights he will probably be best remembered for his curious 'man bun' hair style, and the best bicycle kick goal in Champions League final history (against Liverpool in the 2018 final).

It is imperative that once you start supporting a team you stick with them. If they have a bad run of form and slip down the league table, do not desert them for a better team, cynically swapping clubs in a desperate bid for success. That's the players' job.

TRUE COLOURS

To fully establish your credentials you need to choose a team to support. You can then identify yourself at an early stage in any football conversation as a fan of that club. This will present your companions with an instantly available collection of pre-set comments about your team. In this way football fans avoid the need for such tiresome conventions as having a personality.

It will be far easier to take part in discussions about the current state of football if you pick a team from the Premier League. This is where most media attention is focused.

Geographical proximity is not, contrary to popular opinion, the only acceptable reason for supporting a club. Many fans' allegiances are decided in childhood by quite sentimental factors; they will, for example, pick the team supported by Uncle Alf.

But never confuse being sentimental about the game with trivialising it. Accordingly, you should not use any of the following criteria when deciding which club to support:

- liking the colour of the team's strip;
- fancying the star striker's girlfriend; or
- admiring the star striker's girlfriend's last single.

However your decision is made, it is imperative that once you start supporting a team you stick with them. If they have a bad run of form and slip down the league table, do not desert them for a better team, cynically swapping clubs in a desperate bid for success. That's the players' job.

DISCUSSING YOUR TEAM WITH OTHER SUPPORTERS

The best way to gain acceptance among your fellow fans is by exhibiting a miserable fatalism about your team's chances. Genuine fans care nothing for the cheerily enthusiastic demeanour of those who have jumped on football's bandwagon in recent years. Instead they see their team as a cross to be borne, a spectre which has blighted their lives since childhood, but which nevertheless holds a strange power over them.

The best way to gain acceptance among your fellow fans is by exhibiting a miserable fatalism about your team's chances.

Useful phrases as you discuss your team with a fellow fan include, 'City were useless again on Saturday' (or, in the event of a win, 'City were lucky again on Saturday'); 'We're never going to do anything with Bloggs as manager' (or, if Bloggs has just been replaced,

'We should never have got rid of Bloggs'); and, 'We've got to switch to playing three at the back' (or, if you have been playing three at the back, 'We've got to switch to playing four at the back').

You should find out who your team's local rivals are, so that appropriate venom can be employed when mentioning their name. Newcastle, for example, loathe (and are loathed by) Sunderland. There's not much love lost between Sheffield United and Sheffield Wednesday. Spurs despise Arsenal, and vice-versa. In Bristol the hatred is between Rovers and City. Manchester United's most bitter enemy is Manchester City (and given how deeply the rest of the country dislike them that's saying something). When two local rivals play each other, the match is called a 'derby' – except by the police, who label it a 'threat to public order'.

But sometimes (if rarely) local fans will put aside their differences for the love of the game, demonstrated by the story of the obsessive Newcastle United fan whose long-suffering wife says to him: 'You know, I think you love Newcastle more than you love me.' 'Newcastle?' he replies. 'I love Sunderland more than I love you.'

DISCUSSING FOOTBALL WITH SUPPORTERS OF OTHER TEAMS

As well as following your own club, you need to keep abreast of football in general so that you can discuss the game with fans of other teams.

A cunning approach is to adopt a position on the latest issue that differs from the prevailing wisdom.

Those listening to you will assume that you must know something they don't, and so will take you to be a true expert on the game. It is vital, however, that you refrain from taking this approach too far. You can safely venture the opinion, for instance, that David Beckham was of greater value in central midfield than when playing on the right; but it would be foolhardy to claim that he couldn't hit a barn door from five paces.

TRANSFER RUMOURS

The explosion of media interest in football has meant that broadcasters and newspapers need a constant supply of stories to fill their bulletins, pages and websites. As a result, the slightest rumour, no matter how unlikely, of a particular player being interested in signing for a particular club is pounced upon and disseminated as though it is gospel truth. The advent of Twitter has made this process even more fevered than before.

While 90% of these alleged transfers never stand a chance of actually happening, such is the football fan's capacity for self-deception that he persuades himself that any rumoured transfer of a player to his team is about to be completed within hours. The latest Brazilian World Cup sensation wants to play in Europe? Successful and glamorous clubs like Chelsea and Real Madrid are favourites to complete his signing – but still the Grimsby Town fan holds his breath. After all, a Brazilian wunderkind called Juninho turned up to play more than 100 games for Middlesbrough.

STATISTICS

One device newspapers have adopted in their quest to fill the countless column inches of their football pages is the convoluted use of statistics. In an in-depth analysis of teams' performances, they will compute pieces of information of doubtful relevance like the number of passes completed by a side within their own half compared with the number of passes completed within the opposition's half. You should ignore these statistics. Nowhere in the rules of football does it say that the side completing more passes within their own half shall gain any advantage whatsoever. Ask any Arsenal fan.

SUPERSTITIONS

To exhibit the irrationality that marks the true football fan, you should develop a superstition which you indulge on match days. This is a set routine that you must perform, or an item of clothing you must wear, which once coincided with a victory for your team and which you now repeat in the fear that not doing so will prejudice their chances.

But be careful to pick a superstition that is simple to replicate. It is far easier to rely on the fact that you wore a particular pair of socks when your team won, or that you had Cornflakes rather than Rice Krispies for breakfast, than on the fact that you redecorated your spare room that week.

Clearly, the actions of someone completely unconnected with a team can have no possible effect on that team's performance. The fact that you tap the same lamp post on your way to the ground every week will in no way increase your side's chances of victory. But still you do it. You did it the day 12 years ago when they won 3–0, and have never stopped doing it since. Admittedly, you tell yourself, they have lost many of the subsequent matches. But would they have lost by even more if you hadn't tapped the post? These are the illogical insecurities of the true football fan.

And not just the fan. Players have also become famous for their superstitions. The ex-Manchester United and England star Paul Ince, for example, never put his shirt on until he was running on to the pitch (which is technically a yellow card offence). This explains why he became such a favourite among female fans. Another ex-England footballer with his own curious pre-match ritual was Barry Venison: 'I always used to put my right boot on first, and then obviously my right sock.'

PHRASES

A number of phrases have been used so often in football discussions over the decades that they have taken on the status of cliché. Bluffers should therefore take great care to avoid using any of them, unless you make it abundantly clear that you're being ironic:

'It's a funny old game.'

'We're over the moon.'

'I'm sick as a parrot.'

'It only takes a minute to score a goal.'

'We were robbed' (unless your team were playing in Liverpool, when this will be true in the literal sense).

It is, however, useful to have a stock phrase lined up and ready for use in any conversation about football, such as that used by the erstwhile Coventry, Southampton, Celtic, Middlesbrough and Scotland manager Gordon Strachan: 'Football's a simple game – it's just the players who make it complicated.'

Under no circumstances should you take photos at a match. This will instantly mark you out as a football arriviste of the worst kind.

ATTENDING A MATCH

WHAT TO WEAR

Excessive smartness is the only thing to avoid. Jeans and casual clothing are perfectly acceptable. Many fans wear replica shirts, either in the team's current home strip or their away strip. It is common to have your favourite player's name printed on the back of your shirt, but as modern footballers change clubs more often than they change their socks, this can prove an unwise investment.

To gain credibility, a much more cunning ruse is to wear a shirt from years, if not decades, ago. This implies a lifelong commitment to the club. Such shirts can often be bought from charity shops in the relevant town or city. But take care to buy one a size too small for you, so giving the impression that it has shrunk from years of washing. (Or otherwise ill-fitting due to years of eating too many pies and swilling too many pints of refreshing hop-based libations before, during, and after the game.)

BEFORE THE MATCH

Never get to the match too early. The skilled bluffer will delay arriving at his seat until about three minutes before kick-off. You may think this strange, in that soaking up the atmosphere is presumably a crucial part of any match-day experience. But soaking up beer is a far more crucial part of the match-day experience for regular fans. They are used to the ground, attending it as they do on a fortnightly basis. Consequently, you should attempt to fit in by looking as blasé as possible about the whole experience.

Under no circumstances should you take photos at a match. This will instantly mark you out as a football arriviste of the worst kind.

If you arrive at your seat slightly earlier, you will witness two sights for which it is important to be prepared:

- The first is the players of your team warming up. This will involve them passing the ball to each other, shooting the ball into the net from 30 yards out, and running together in a coordinated and organised manner. None of these things will happen during the match.

- The second sight for which you must be prepared is the mascot. This will be an out-of-work actor dressed as a garishly coloured animal of the farmyard, jungle or imaginary variety. Many people would be fazed by a seven-foot purple chimpanzee.

The bluffer is not. You will join in with the spirit of things, laughing good-naturedly as the mascot makes insulting gestures at the opposition fans – or has a fight with the opposing team's mascot. (Few sights are more entertaining than two grown men dressed as birds laying into each other.)

Having warmed up, the players return to their dressing rooms and prepare for the match proper. This is where the atmosphere really builds up, and as the teams run out, the home fans cheer their side in an attempt to intimidate the opposition. Clubs also play music to aid this process. Crystal Palace, for instance, run out to 'Glad All Over' by the Dave Clark Five – a triumph of hope over expectation if ever there was one.

Another tradition at this point is for fans to throw torn-up tickets into the air, as a sort of football confetti. If their team has been on a particularly bad run of form, season ticket holders have been known to tear up the ticket for next week's match.

FOOTBALL KIT

Wherever you're watching football, different makes of shirts, shorts and boots will be on display. This provides an opportunity for you to reveal your knowledge about the various kit brands and how they got their names. You can guarantee that at least one of the following brands will feature in any match you see, so becoming familiar with them will provide significant bluffing potential:

Umbro Supplier of kit to many leading nations and clubs (for instance, Manchester City won their 2012 Premier League title wearing Umbro shirts). The name derives from the firm's founding in 1924 by the Humphreys brothers Harold and Wallace, in Cheshire. The latter has now slipped to second in the list of Most Famous People Called Wallace from the North-west of England.

Adidas founded in 1948 by the German Adi (Adolf) Dassler, after he fell out with his brother and partner Rudolf, with whom he'd been running an existing sportswear company.

Puma Not to be outdone, Rudolf Dassler formed his own company to compete with Adidas. At first he followed the pattern of using the first few letters of each name, and called it Ruda. Soon, however, he looked to the world of speedy animals for inspiration, and chose the name by which his firm would become famous. Just think, if the two brothers had got together, they could have set out to conquer the world. It's in the national psyche.

Nike Pronounced 'nye-key' in the USA and by the company itself, but often rhymed with 'bike' in the UK. An American sportswear company named after the Greek goddess of victory. Its famous 'Swoosh' logo was designed in 1971 by a graphic design student doing some freelance work for Nike's founder, Phil Knight. She was paid $35 (although Knight later gave her some shares in the company as extra payment). At the time, Knight said of the logo: 'I don't love it, but maybe it will grow on me.' By 2012 his holding in Nike gave him a personal fortune of $14.4bn. It must be assumed that the Swoosh has grown on him quite a lot by now.

ASICS The name stands for 'anima sana in corpore sano', a variation on the Latin phrase that means 'a healthy mind in a healthy body'. Yet more influence from the classics. Players who are seldom famed for their literacy are running around wearing kit plastered in Ancient Greek and Latin.

NICKNAMES

Every football club has at least one nickname, and by using some of these you'll demonstrate your familiarity with the sport. It is always a good idea therefore to find out in advance the nickname of the opposing team, so that you can say knowledgeably, for example: 'That's the problem with the "Nobblers". No finesse, and too much reliance on kicking opposition players out of the game.' Some nicknames are straightforward – 'the Reds', 'the Blues', 'the Claret and Blues', 'the Sky Blues', 'the Black and Blues' (that's either Inter Milan or a team regularly getting a good kicking). Others, though, have more intriguing origins:

Arsenal *'The Gunners'*; has its origins in the club's first home south of the Thames near Woolwich Arsenal. The club's crest features a cannon. Until 1925 this pointed to the right, from 1925 until 2002 to the left, and since 2002 to the right again. A useful bit of satire to chuck in whenever their goalie dives the wrong way for a penalty.

Everton *'The Toffees'*; so called because the club used to hire someone to throw complimentary toffees into the crowd before a game. Or there was a toffee shop near the ground. Take your pick.

Bristol Rovers *'The Gas'*; Rovers' old ground, Eastville, was next to a gasworks. The name was originated by fans of local rivals Bristol City as a term of abuse, but Rovers supporters have adopted it as a badge of pride.

Walsall *'The Saddlers'*; links to the local saddle-making industry.

Norwich City *'The Canaries'*; the team wear bright yellow. That's about it.

Ipswich Town *'The Tractor Boys'*; a less-than-respectful reference by opposition fans to the largely agriculturally employed nature of the club's supporter base. Sensibly, the Ipswich fans have adopted it with gusto.

West Bromwich Albion *'The Baggies'*; the club was originally the works team of a local iron foundry whose staff wore trousers known as 'baggies'. Or the name given to the huge bags used to collect the money from ticket sales. Again, take your pick.

Charlton Athletic *'The Addicks'*; their players used to love eating haddock, and also offered it to their opponents after matches in a show of hospitality.

Barnsley *'The Tykes'*; apparently a nickname for Yorkshiremen.

West Ham United *'The Irons'*; a reference to the club's origins as the team of Thames Ironworks Ltd. Also known as 'The Hammers' (although this apparently has nothing to do with the club's location).

Watford *'The Hornets'*; the team strip is red and yellow.

Bury *'The Shakers'*; before Bury played Blackburn Rovers in the 1892 Lancashire Cup Final, their chairman J.T. Ingham said: 'We shall shake 'em!' They duly did (winning by a comfortable margin), and the name stuck. Another gem to throw in whenever Bury are mentioned is that their name ('Bury', not their nickname) is the shortest of any of the top 92 English clubs.

DURING THE MATCH

Apart from the 22 players, there will be a number of other personnel involved in proceedings:

The referee

This is an officious-looking individual, normally dressed in black, who runs around in the middle of the play and blows his whistle at apparently random intervals.

There are several items a referee must take on to the pitch with him: a watch, a notebook (with red and yellow cards), a whistle, and a complete refusal to believe that he is not the sole reason everyone has turned up to watch the match.

The linesmen

These are the two men, sometimes women, with flags who run up and down the touchlines, aiding the referee on decisions. Most of these will be about offside, and thus complete guesswork, but they also help out on other matters. For instance, throw-ins; the linesman will wait to see who picks up the ball to take the throw, and then quickly point his flag in the appropriate direction as though he knew all along which player the ball had come off.

In the late 1990s the game's authorities renamed linesmen 'assistant referees'. The bluffer should not use this preposterous term; no one else does. Not even linesmen.

The fourth official

This self-regarding individual patrols the area near the managers' dugouts, in case they have the impertinence to question any of the referee or linesmen's decisions. His main role is to get his 'hair dried' (*see* 'Glossary') by the two managers and their acolytes, and to shrug his shoulders in what is meant to be a 'Not my decision, mate' sort of way. In fact, it is unlikely that any fourth official in their short history in the game has ever attempted to overturn a match referee's decision. Thus their only practical role is to hold up the electronic board to indicate how many minutes of extra time are to be added. Occasionally they also try to use the same boards to signify the shirt numbers of players involved in a substitution. They rarely get this right.

The manager

The manager is easy to recognise as he will be the only one in the dugout wearing a suit. (Unless his job has been under threat recently, in which case he will be wearing a tracksuit to imply solidarity with 'the lads').

The typical manager will spend the entire match pacing up and down the touchline, shouting furious instructions to his players despite the fact that none of them stand a chance of hearing anything above the noise of the crowd. Even if they could, none of them would have a clue what he was going on about. The undeniable, but nevertheless touching, futility of this practice provides a metaphor for football as a whole.

The goalkeeping coach

This coach has nothing to do with the goalkeeper. His job is to sit next to the manager on the bench assuring him that his convictions about the referee being biased are indeed correct.

Ball boys

Ball boys and girls are positioned around the edge of the pitch and are there to return the ball quickly to the players. Unless, of course, the players they are meant to return the ball to belong to the opposition team. Then they will delay the return of the ball until they receive a signal from the home bench to indicate that their team is back in position. All footballers are introduced to this sort of gamesmanship from an early age.

Stadium announcer

The announcer usually runs the area's fifth-best mobile disco, and has microphone skills to match. Never expect to understand a single word uttered by the announcer.

HOW TO BEHAVE

Take your cues from your fellow fans. Cheer, jeer, laugh, applaud, etc., when they do. Don't worry if you can't work out why a referee has given a particular decision. Very often he won't know either. Just make the same noises as the people around you. If in doubt the exclamation 'Unbelievable!', accompanied by a shake of the head, is always a usefully ambiguous observation about most things.

Don't be surprised when a player appeals for (say) a throw-in when the ball has clearly come off his own shin rather than his opponent's. This is not cheating. It's another example of gamesmanship. Everyone in the game of football engages in it, including supporters who will be claiming the same thing, but more volubly.

Don't be surprised when a player appeals for a throw-in when the ball has clearly come off his own shin.

Equally, you must accept that football supporters are fickle creatures. If a player who has been having an awful game and attracting the condemnation of his fans suddenly scores the winning goal, he will instantly become the best player in the world and his name will be chanted in glowing terms for the rest of the match.

- If your team scores, go into raptures of joy.
- If the opposition scores, look stunned and disbelieving.

Either way, you will get to witness professional footballers' goal celebrations. Once a simple case of the firm, manly handshake before returning to the centre circle for the restart, these have now become choreographed epics of which Busby Berkeley would be proud. Teams spend hours on the training ground perfecting their celebration routines, ignoring the fact that if they spent the same amount of time practising their football they might actually have a few more goals to celebrate.

CHANTING

Throughout the match there will be chanting. It is advisable to join in. You needn't feel self-conscious about every other word you utter being an obscenity. Normal rules do not apply inside football grounds. You will pick up most of your team's chants as you go along. But as a general rule about what to expect, they usually fall into four groups:

Chants directed at your own side

These will normally (though not always) be supportive. Most teams have a version of the 'Greatest Team' chant, which is sung to the tune of 'The Wild Rover':

'And it's Stockport County, Stockport County FC,
We're by far the greatest team the world has ever seen.'

This is patently absurd. Passionate as the supporters of Stockport County undoubtedly are, not even they would claim (in their more lucid moments) that their team is better than, for instance, the legendary Brazil side that swept all before them in the 1970 World Cup. But an absence of logical reasoning is one of football fans' most endearing traits.

Chants directed at the opposition

If your team is losing, it is customary to chant at the opposition fans (to the tune of 'Guantanamera'):

'Sing when you're winning,
You only sing when you're winning,
Sing when you're win–ning…'

If your team is winning, a common chant is (to the tune of 'Bread of Heaven'):

'Can we play you, can we play you,
Can we play you every week?'

Chants directed at the referee

These will question his eyesight, his parentage, or his propensity for having sex on a regular basis (with himself).

Great historical chants

As well as joining in with chants during the match, you're advised to have a few favourite chants from the past ready for when talk in the pub turns to this subject. We recommend the following:

When the Rangers goalkeeper Andy Goram was diagnosed with mild schizophrenia, opposition fans sang: 'Two Andy Gorams, there's only two Andy Gorams....'

When Scotland played in Italy, the away fans chanted 'Deep-fry your pizzas, we're going to deep-fry your pizzas.'

Manchester United fans used to chant (to the tune of 'Oops Upside Your Head') 'Ooh, aah, Cantona.' When Frenchman Eric Cantona was banned for nine months for assaulting a Crystal Palace fan, the supporters of Leeds United (fierce enemies of the Manchester club, and the club that had sold Cantona to them), sang 'Où est Cantona?' Bilingual chanting – you have to doff your beret to that.

Also in the 'turning-an-existing-chant-on-its-head' tradition, Brighton and Hove Albion fans started singing about their beloved striker Bobby Zamora (to the tune of 'That's Amore' by Dean Martin): 'When the ball hits the goal, it's not Shearer or Cole, it's Zamora.' When Zamora played for Fulham, on the other hand, and was struggling to score, fans (including the home ones) sang: 'When the ball hits his head, and it lands in row Z, that's Zamora.'

SKILLS TO WATCH FOR

The real skills that characterise professional football are not the ones you might expect – ball control, speed, passing accuracy, the ability to turn quickly, etc. Instead they include:

Play-acting Players routinely pretend that they have been fouled in order to win free kicks and get their opponents booked. The standards of acting used to achieve this are at times so excellent that theatrical agents have been known to attend some Premier League matches looking for talent. But more often than not, players' efforts in the dramatic arts are woefully inadequate, and there are tell-tale signs that give this away, e.g.:

- the 'transferred pain syndrome', for example, where someone gets lightly tapped on the shoulder, but falls to the ground clutching his face as if in agony; and

- the 'Lazarus effect', in which a player somehow achieves a miraculous recovery the very instant the referee awards a free kick in his favour.

Acrobatics A favourite is the 'stepladder', where a player stands behind an opponent, lifting himself up on his shoulders to head the ball first.

Observation The skill of estimating when a ball is at the top of its flight after a long clearance from the goalkeeper. This enables the player to elbow his marker out of the way while attention is diverted.

Beating your opponent The skill that sometimes means getting away from him while retaining control of the ball. Often, however, it has a more literal meaning.

SCREEN PLAY

Even if you can gain admission to the match of your choice, watching the game on a big screen in a pub has a number of advantages. It's warmer, it's cheaper (a couple of pints will cost you a fraction of the average Premier League ticket price), and you don't have to sit in a motorway hold-up at nine o'clock on a Saturday night, punching the dashboard in frustration at the last-minute chance your team missed that would have won them the match. But you should be aware of the rules:

1. If you are on your own and your team scores, do not jump up in the air and shout at the top of your voice. This runs the risk of offending any opposition fans present who might interpret your reaction as a deliberate provocation. Instead, clench your fist tightly and growl a muted 'yes' through gritted teeth, as though this was an involuntary action by someone who nevertheless wishes to preserve their public dignity.

2. If you are watching the match with a friend, you should develop the ability to talk out of the corner of your mouth. This is because your eyes must never leave the match. Football fans in pubs thus take on the appearance of undercover cops in a crowded square – communicating, but not actually acknowledging each other's presence.

3. The same rule applies when being served at the bar. You can allow yourself the briefest break from watching the match in order to achieve eye contact with the bar staff, but after that you must complete the rest of the transaction while remaining glued to the screen. Offer your money and receive your change simply by holding out your hand; make their hand come to yours, not vice-versa. Only check your change during a break in play.

4. Accept that if you go to the Gents, someone will score a leading contender for 'Goal of the Season'. If you put off your visit, the game will remain goalless. There is no escaping this immutable law of football.

If your team is not involved in the match, there are some simple guidelines that tell you who to support:

   a. If Manchester United are playing, support the other team.
   b. If an English team other than Manchester United are playing in a European competition, support the English team.

c.   If Manchester United are playing in a European competition, grudgingly support them, but pepper your support with comments about their Surrey fan base.

d.   If it's an international match involving England, support England.

e.   If it's an international match not involving England, support anyone except Germany.

f.   If you're in a strange town, support the team everyone else in the pub is supporting.

The philosopher John Stuart Mill wrote about the importance of pursuing your own individualist agenda, free from the tyranny of popular opinion. As and when John Stuart Mill has supported Sheffield United in a pub full of Sheffield Wednesday fans, you can listen to him.

ACTION REPLAYS

These are a vital part of TV coverage of football. They allow the director to play back an interesting or controversial incident, thereby ensuring that you miss the goal someone has gone on to score directly from the event in question. A particular version of the action replay is the 'VAR' ('Video Assistant Referee') system. This has been used by the game's authorities to settle contentious moments during play: the referee has access, via a headset, to someone off the field who can review an incident and advise on which decision to make. Different systems have been proposed and trialled in different countries, reflecting contrasting views on how extensive the technology's role should be. For example, should VAR be used to decide whether it's a corner or a goalkick, or should it be restricted to more important incidents like penalties? A limited version of VAR was tested in English FA Cup (not league) matches in the 2017-18 season. Within minutes fans were yelling that it was ruining the flow of matches, as referees stood around for minutes at a time waiting for their off-field adviser to come back to them. These are the same fans who had spent decades yelling that it was mad how TV viewers could see instantly that a goal should have been disallowed while the referee wasn't allowed access to the same footage. Bluffers will shake their heads wearily and say that there is, in short, no pleasing a football fan.

TV PUNDITS

A crucial difference between attending a match in person and watching it in the pub is that in the latter case you can listen to the analysis provided by the television pundits (if the sound is turned up sufficiently). These strange creatures come in a variety of species – professional presenters, ex-managers, ex-players, currently injured players…the list is endless, and quite often tedious. Some, such as the BBC's Mark Lawrenson (who played for Liverpool in the 1980s), are determined to display their cynicism about the modern game at every possible opportunity. Others, especially those who have played the game more recently (so earning vastly more money), give off a *Great Gatsby*-esque air of ennui, not just about the game of football they're watching that minute, but about the whole notion of a lifetime ahead of them with nothing more to animate it than whether they should drive the Bentley or the Porsche today. This makes them just as spirit-sapping to listen to as you'd expect.

Reserve your praise for the odd pundit such as Sky's Gary Neville (ex-England and Man Utd) or ITV's Lee Dixon (ex-England and Arsenal) or BBC *Match of the Day*'s Danny Murphy (ex England and Liverpool), all of whom display a keen knowledge of and interest in the modern game, and who don't talk in clichés like most of their contemporaries. Otherwise, you should state that pundits are there not to inform viewers, but to entertain them. In some cases this will be as a result of their choice of suit, in others by their use of grammatical constructions with which they are clearly unfamiliar, and in yet others by their failure to get to grips with technological wizardry intended to aid their analysis. This has become ever more sophisticated in recent seasons, but almost always ends up with the pundit drawing white lines on the screen to illustrate the player and/or ball movements under discussion. These lines are similar to the arrows in the opening credits of *Dad's Army,* except that they have marginally less meaning.

PLAYER INTERVIEWS

Post-match player interviews are yet another delight that you miss out on by actually bothering to attend a match. Footballers being creatures of habit, the same phrases tend to crop up again and again, so it is imperative that the bluffer is familiar with them. For example:

'It was a game of two halves.' This means that the pattern of play before half-time was markedly different from that after the break. Footballers should not be mocked for using this cliché. In their terms, the concept of two halves adding up to a whole constitutes advanced mathematics.

'We set out our stall early doors.' We showed the other team that we were determined to win the game at an early stage.

'We came to do a job.' This means the same as 'We came to play a game of football.'

'Obviously.' Players have started using this as a generic verbal fill-in, rather like 'um' and 'er'. They say it about things that are the exact opposite of obvious. 'Well, you know, obviously in the dressing room at half-time the gaffer told us to feed the ball more down the left.' (How is that obvious to anyone other than those in the dressing room at the time?)

Do not think badly of players for constantly falling back on stock expressions. It's infinitely preferable to what can come out of their mouths when they ad-lib:

'We're in a no-win situation, except if we win we'll go through to the next round.' Graeme Le Saux

On moving to Italy: 'It was like living in a different country.' Ian Rush

'I don't want to see him [Rooney] leaving these shores, but if he does I think he'll be going abroad.' Ian Wright

'If you stand still there's only one way to go, and that's backwards.' Peter Shilton

'Football's football; if that weren't the case then it wouldn't be the game that it is.' Garth Crooks

'Arsenal are streets ahead of everyone in this league and Manchester United are up there with them.'
Craig Bellamy

'You need at least eight or nine men in a ten-man wall.'
Mark Lawrenson

'I'd been ill and hadn't trained for a week and I'd been out of the team for three weeks before that, so I wasn't sharp. I got cramp before half-time as well. But I'm not one to make excuses.' Clinton Morrison

'Gary Neville was captain, and now Ryan Giggs has taken on the mantelpiece.' Rio Ferdinand

There's no point in pretending that you know everything about football – nobody does – but if you've got this far and you've absorbed at least a modicum of the information and advice contained within these pages, then you will almost certainly know more than 99% of the rest of the human race about what football is, how it is played, who plays it, who watches it, and why they watch it. What you now do with this information is up to you, but here's a suggestion: be confident about your new-found knowledge, see how far it takes you, but above all have fun using it.

And if you remember only one thing to drop into any conversation about football's rightful place in the history of popular culture, remember the famous words of the legendary Liverpool manager Bill Shankly: 'Football is not a matter of life and death – it's much more important than that.'

GLOSSARY

Ajax One of the great teams of European football, from Amsterdam, pronounced 'Eye-acks', and not like the cleaning powder 'Ay-jacks', or indeed the mythological Greek warrior 'Ay-ash'.

Back-heel Clever way of passing the ball that catches your opponents unawares. Usually it comes off the side rather than the back of the heel, giving your opponents a throw-in they weren't expecting.

Bicycle-kick The act of somersaulting backwards to kick the ball while your foot is up in the air. When performed by a professional it often wins 'Goal of the Month'. When performed in your local park it usually results in concussion or a broken neck.

Bonus The financial reward, over and above their normal salary, offered to players if they perform well (by winning a match, scoring a certain number of goals, etc.). A less conventional bonus was offered by Turkish belly dancer Sether Seniz who allegedly offered to sleep with any member of her national team who scored a goal against West Germany. Strangely, the defenders were far less happy about this proposal than the attacking players.

Cabbage patch A muddy, uneven pitch. When your team loses on a cabbage patch, the game should never have gone ahead. When they win, it was the same for both sides.

Diving A dramatic feat of agility practised by strikers in the opposition penalty area, designed to trick referees into thinking they have been brutally scythed down by psychotic defenders. The expressions 'dying swan routine' and 'Oscar-winning performance' have been popularised as a means of describing this technique, best exemplified by German forward Jürgen Klinsmann who endeared himself to supporters the world over by making a dive part of his goal celebrations. (And who said Germans couldn't do irony?)

Donkey An ineffective player.

Early bath An expression that describes the premature departure of a player from the field for misconduct.

Feint Tricking a defender by pretending to kick the ball one way, then quickly kicking it another. Astonishingly, highly paid professional footballers still fall for this old ruse, week in, week out.

Fifty-fifty ball A ball that two players, one from each side, have an equal chance of reaching. Also so called because more often than not both of them will need 50 stitches in their head wounds after the challenge.

Goalhanger A forward player who 'hangs' around the opposition's goal in the hope of tapping in a loose ball without contributing much else to the game. Also known as a 'poacher' or a 'Lineker'.

Hairdryer The term for an effective means of communication with an underperforming player, invented by the former Manchester United manager Sir Alex Ferguson. It involves getting up close and personal with the player and shouting so loud that the force of your breath dries their hair.

Handbags at dawn An expression describing the spectacle of two players squaring up and threatening each other with violence. It is a parody of the notion of a gentlemen's duel with pistols. Sometimes just referred to as 'handbags'.

In the hole An attacking position just behind the main strikers. Usually occupied by someone who plays as if he's stuck in one.

Man-marking A defensive system wherein you are allocated one particular opponent to track for the entire match. Usually involves whispered compliments on the quality of his wife's breakfasts.

Nutmeg The act of playing the ball between an opponent's legs. Seen as the ultimate insult. If you insist on playing park football, under no circumstances nutmeg anyone. If it happens by mistake, prebook your ambulance there and then.

On a free Transfer of a player from one club to another while he's out of contract, so no fee applies. Nothing else about modern football is free, at least not for the fan.

One-two Receiving the ball from a teammate and playing it immediately back to him as he quickly moves to a new position. Even more complicated passing manoeuvres would be possible if footballers could count any higher than two.

Pen Abbreviation for 'penalty', the only kind of pen with which most professional footballers have any familiarity.

Pickles The dog who found the stolen World Cup trophy in a hedge, shortly before the 1966 tournament. As a reward, he was allowed to lick the plates clean after England's victory banquet. Many of the English team's subsequent World Cup campaigns have also been associated with the phrase 'dog's dinner'.

Reading the game Anticipating the imminent movements of other players to give you a competitive advantage. For many players it is the only type of reading they do, apart from Twitter.

Rotation system Tactic by which a manager can annoy a different group of players every week by leaving them on the substitutes' bench.

Sick as a parrot Time-honoured footballing expression for a state of mind that is less-than-brimming with joy. Etymological origin uncertain.

Total football A system pioneered by the great Holland team of the 1970s, where conventional formations were abandoned in favour of excellence all over the pitch. Not to be confused with the England system which is total something else.

Triple somersault What a player performs if an opposition defender so much as nudges him in the penalty area.

Upright Common term for a goalpost. Little else in the modern game merits the use of this word.

A BIT MORE BLUFFING...

Bluffer's® GUIDE TO BREXIT

Bluffer's® GUIDE TO CRICKET

Bluffer's® GUIDE TO MANAGEMENT

Bluffer's® GUIDE TO CYCLING

Bluffer's® GUIDE TO SOCIAL MEDIA

Bluffer's® GUIDE TO ETIQUETTE

Bluffer's® GUIDE TO RACING

Bluffer's® GUIDE TO GOLF

Bluffer's® GUIDE TO WINE

Bluffer's® GUIDE TO JAZZ

Bluffer's® GUIDE TO DOGS

Bluffer's® GUIDE TO FISHING

Bluffer's® GUIDE TO OPERA

Bluffer's® GUIDE TO CHOCOLATE

Bluffer's® GUIDE TO CATS

Bluffer's® GUIDE TO BEER

Bluffer's® GUIDE TO QUANTUM UNIVERSE

Bluffer's® GUIDE TO FOOTBALL

Bluffer's® GUIDE TO RUGBY

Bluffer's® GUIDE TO SKIING

Available from all good bookshops

bluffers.com